10

MINUTE
CHINESE
Takeout

KWOKLYN WAN

Publishing Director Sarah Lavelle
Editor Stacey Cleworth
Editorial Assistant Sofie Shearman
Art Direction and Design Emily Lapworth
Photographer Sam Folan
Food Stylist Katie Marshall
Props Stylist Agathe Gits
Head of Production Stephen Lang
Production Controller Sabeena Atchia

Published in 2022 by Quadrille
an imprint of Hardie Grant Publishing

Quadrille
52–54 Southwark Street
London SE1 1UN
quadrille.com

Cataloguing in Publication Data: a catalogue record
for this book is available from the British Library.

ISBN 9781787137431

Printed in China

10 MINUTE CHINESE Takeout

KWOKLYN WAN

SIMPLE, CLASSIC DISHES READY IN JUST 10 MINUTES!

Photography by Sam Folan

Hardie Grant

QUADRILLE

SOUPS & SNACKS

VEGETABLES

SEAFOOD

MEAT

CHICKEN & DUCK

44.

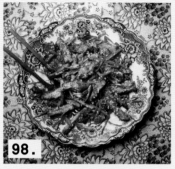

98.

NOODLES & RICE

81.

154.

INTRODUCTION

As I began researching 'express' Chinese recipes I stumbled upon my family's restaurant archives and uncovered some amazing 'retro' dishes that had once graced the menu in my grandad's restaurant back in the sixties and seventies. I also took plenty of inspiration from dishes that members of my extended family were cooking on a day-to-day basis, as these were all super-easy and very, VERY quick to cook while never sacrificing flavour in the pursuit of speed.

Unlike the kitchen in a busy takeout or restaurant, a home kitchen should be a place of calm where you can enjoy the time you take preparing your ingredients, a place where you can sing along to your favourite tunes as you dance them into the wok and find your state of zen as you elevate finished dishes to your serving plate to the awe of your family and guests ...

Reality check! Between juggling full-time jobs, busy family schedules, pets, fitness and household chores, most of us are lucky if we find time midweek to boil some dried noodles and toss in a shop-bought sauce. Sure, the weekend can be a sacred time when you enjoy preparing banquet-style feasts, but that doesn't mean your taste buds have to go on a five-day flavour fast! This book is going to show you just how easy it is to get your Chinese takeout fix faster than popping a ready meal in the microwave. All the flavour, none of the nasties and barely a dent in your busy day; I've got you covered from breakfast till supper with soups and snacks that will have everyone drooling, tips and tricks on getting the best out of a selection of ready-prepared and cooked ingredients, and simple fail-safe flavour combinations that can be used time and again with your meat, fish or veg of choice.

Give them a try and always remember this: the recipe is your guide, but your own taste is key to creating truly mouth-watering dishes, so always taste, season and taste again!

I would love to hear about the recipes you've been trying and you can watch me cooking more dishes, as well as keeping up to date with my food adventures at: www.kwoklynwan.com.

COOKING TECHNIQUES

Tenderizing/Velveting

Although the recipes in this book are all about speed, I've included this technique because it's recommended (but not essential) if you've got a bit of time. If you've ever wondered why meat or fish served in a Chinese takeaway or restaurant is so tender and juicy, 'velveting' is the reason. This marinating technique makes it harder for the proteins on the surface to bond, therefore keeping it tender and juicier during cooking. To marinate 350–600g (12oz–21oz) meat or fish you will need:

1 tbsp Chinese rice wine (Shaoxing wine), or use water
1 tbsp cornflour (cornstarch)
1 tbsp dark soy sauce
1 tbsp light soy sauce
1 tsp bicarbonate of soda (baking soda)

Put all the ingredients into a large bowl along with the sliced meat, fish or king prawns (jumbo shrimp). Using your hands, mix everything together for around 30–45 seconds; there should be no liquid left sitting in the bottom of the bowl by the time you've finished mixing. Cover the bowl and set aside for ideally 2 hours before cooking.

Blanching

Blanching, or partially cooking some of the larger ingredients, usually vegetables, before tossing them into your wok will save time and also ensure they are tender and cooked through. This method also ensures that the other ingredients are not overcooked, as the pre-blanched ingredients need less time in the wok. Simply plunge the vegetables into boiling water for a brief time and then drain.

Shallow-frying

This method is used in many restaurants and takeaways around the world to cook pieces of meat or vegetables until crisp before adding them to a rich sauce. You generally need about 250ml (1 cup) of a neutral oil, added to a hot wok so that the food cooks quickly and evenly.

Stir-frying

The key to a great stir-fry is the size of your ingredients; this cooking method is very quick, so you need to make sure your ingredients, whether raw or pre-cooked, are all bite-sized and approximately the same size as each other to result in even cooking.

Simply toss your ingredients into the wok with a little oil, add your seasoning and within mere minutes you will have a delicious dish ready for serving. Vegetables will retain their bright, colourful, crisp textures, while meats will be tender, caramelized and juicy.

Thickening

Chinese cuisine is well known for its velvety sauces that cling to each ingredient as they spill onto your plate. Creating a rich, smooth sauce isn't as hard as it may seem; simply adding a thickening agent during the cooking process will achieve this. For me, the thickening agent of choice has always been cornflour, added into marinades or sauce mixes, or even towards the very end of the cooking process, mixed with a little bit of water to add a final touch of velvet to a dish.

STORE CUPBOARD INGREDIENTS

Chinese food is traditionally categorized into five flavours: **Salty, Spicy, Sour, Sweet** and **Bitter**, with a sixth taste more recently coming to the fore, **Umami**. Your store cupboard needs to provide you with these elements to enable you to create not just tasty food but outstanding dishes that tickle each individual taste bud.

You'll find most of these ingredients in larger supermarkets, Asian supermarkets or online.

Oil

There are a multitude of oils to choose from, including vegetable, coconut, groundnut (peanut), sunflower, rapeseed (canola) and olive. For Chinese cooking, the oil you choose needs to be able to be used for stir-frying but should also not deteriorate or 'lose power' (as my dad would say) when used to shallow or deep-fry. For this reason, I mostly use vegetable, sunflower or groundnut.

A note on used oil: Shallow- or deep-frying are excellent when you're against the clock, but they do require the use of more oil than a quick stir-fry. To save wastage, once your used oil has completely cooled, use a fine sieve to remove any debris and decant the oil into a bottle or jar to be used again. In the restaurants and takeaways I've worked, we would use the oil three or four times before discarding it completely. By re-using oil, you'll also be injecting extra flavour into the dishes you cook with the essence of the ingredients that graced the wok before.

Sesame oil

I know I must sound like a broken record, but you should **never** fry with sesame oil, as once heated it begins to lose its amazing flavour. Drizzle sesame oil over a dish to inject an aromatic nutty flavour at the end of cooking or add it to marinades. Where possible only ever use pure sesame oil and not the blended version, which is much less flavoursome.

Light soy sauce

This ingredient is used extensively in Chinese cookery, with the light version being used predominantly to season the dish. Those who are gluten-intolerant will be pleased to know that there are wheat-free brands available.

Dark soy sauce

Dark soy sauce is not as salty as its lighter sibling and is used for adding a rich caramel colour to dishes along with its deep umami flavour.

Salt

One of the five key elements of flavour in Chinese cookery, salt is a simple yet essential seasoning tool. As everyone's taste will differ, I always recommend the 'taste first, then season' approach to avoid under- or over-salting your food; what's tasty for me might be far too salty for you. A popular Chinese saying springs to mind: 'Eating is as important as breathing, as we cannot live without food, so let's make it the best we can.'

Sugar

Sugar is often used in Chinese cuisine to not only sweeten and balance a dish but also to enhance the texture of sauces; by adding a little sugar, the viscosity of the sauce changes, increasing the length of time on the palate as we eat.

White pepper

White pepper is used more commonly than black pepper in Chinese restaurants and takeaways, added to inject a subtle warm glow and background heat to a dish. It is usually found as a ready-ground powder.

Oyster sauce or mushroom stir-fry sauce

Invented by accident in 1888, oyster sauce is an ingredient that since its inception has gone on to become a game-changer. Packed with umami saltiness, this sauce can be added to any dish to enhance its flavour.

Mushroom stir-fry sauce is very similar to oyster sauce in texture and usage; made from dried shiitake (poku) mushrooms and seaweed, it still packs that rich umami flavour and is a great alternative for vegetarians.

Rice vinegar

Used to inject a sour note into any dish, sometimes a splash is all you need for a subtle kick; other times a full cup might be used to give the dish a real tangy punch.

Chinese black rice vinegar (Chinkiang)

With a more complex, slightly smoky flavour this makes a great addition to dipping sauces and noodle broths.

Chinese rice wine (Shaoxing wine)

The fermented pungent note of Chinese rice wine is unique (though for a more subtle alcoholic note, you can use dry sherry or even red wine instead). It is used in marinades or at the end of the cooking process and it really does transform the dish to another level.

Chinese yellow bean sauce

Sometimes labelled as 'yellow bean paste', this basic staple of any Chinese store cupboard is a fermented soybean purée that is mixed with flour, salt, sugar and water or soy sauce to provide a perfect base for a wide range of sauces.

Cornflour (cornstarch)

This ingredient is vital to any Chinese kitchen; it's used to thicken sauces, to tenderize meats before cooking or to coat chopped vegetables or meat before frying to create the crispiest of batters.

Fermented chilli bean paste (doubanjiang)

Doubanjiang is characteristically used in Sichuan cuisine. Made from fermented broad beans, chillies and soybeans it brings a deep complex umami flavour and a hearty kick from the chillies.

FRESH AND FROZEN INGREDIENTS

When it comes to preparing a quick meal, having ready-prepared ingredients to hand can be a blessing. Most supermarkets now stock an amazing array of pre-prepared vegetables in the fresh produce sections, from diced onions to sliced carrots, not forgetting the ample selections of canned veggies and ready-to-wok noodles and rice. Garlic and ginger – two ingredients that are used extensively in these recipes – can also be found ready-puréed, but a word to the wise: some (but not all) jar varieties contain vinegar, which can impact on the seasoning of a dish; however, there are also squeezy tubes to choose from so go with whatever suits your own palate.

If you're a daily fresh veg eater, the produce section may be your go-to zone for ready-prepared vegetables but don't underestimate the value of the freezer. The frozen food sections in supermarkets now have a vast array of prepared veg, so you can turn your freezer into a treasure trove of those not-so-frequently used ingredients, while still retaining all of the colour and vitamins you'd expect to find in the fresh veg. Cut down on your food waste and save money at the same time by buying fresh when you know you're going to use the whole packet, and going frozen for items you'll need to store for longer.

SOUPS & SNACKS

CANTONESE-STYLE EGGS

Forget everything you think you know about scrambled eggs! With a smooth richness that only the inclusion of lard can provide, these velvety smooth eggs are delicately flavoured with classic Cantonese aromats and then quickly transformed into a substantial snack by the hunks of smoky hot dog.

4 MINUTES   **6 MINUTES**   **SERVES 2**

3 hot dogs, cut into bite-sized pieces
3 spring onions (scallions), cut into
  2cm (¾in) slices
5 eggs
½ tsp salt
½ tsp sugar
1 tsp Chinese rice wine
  (Shaoxing wine)
1 tsp sesame oil
1 tsp cornflour (cornstarch)
  mixed with 2 tsp water
1 tsp chicken powder (optional)
pinch of white pepper
2 tbsp lard

Place a non-stick wok over a medium heat; when hot add the hot dog pieces and spring onions (scallions) and cook for 1–2 minutes. Remove from the wok and set aside.

Break the eggs into a bowl and whisk vigorously until bubbles are visible on top of the eggs. At this point you can add your salt, sugar, rice wine, sesame oil, cornflour (cornstarch) mixture, chicken powder, white pepper and finally your cooked hot dog pieces and spring onions. Give everything a good mix.

Place your wok back over a medium-high heat and add the lard; once it has melted and is nearly at smoking point, pour in your egg mixture. Lift the wok off the heat and use a spoon to pull the cooked curds to the side of the wok, allowing the loose egg mixture to pool in the middle of the wok. Place the wok back over the heat and, when more curds start to form, repeat the process of moving away from the heat and scooping the eggs to the side. You don't want to overcook the eggs so cook just until some wet curds remain. Once the eggs are no longer pooling, remove from the wok and transfer to a plate.

KING PRAWN & SPINACH SOUP

A deeply umami bowl of soup that not only delivers on clean, fresh flavour but also boasts a whole host of vitamins and minerals, providing you with an effortlessly delicious health kick.

1 MINUTE   **5 MINUTES**   **SERVES 2**

1 litre (4 cups) dashi stock
2 tsp light soy sauce
1 tbsp Chinese rice wine
   (Shaoxing wine)
6 large king prawns (jumbo shrimp),
   peeled and deveined
60g (2½oz) fresh spinach
pinch of bonito fish flakes

Pour your dashi stock, soy sauce and rice wine into a saucepan and gently bring to the boil.

Bring another saucepan of water to the boil, add the prawns (jumbo shrimp) and simmer for 1–2 minutes – just until they have turned pink and are cooked. Remove with a slotted spoon, then add the spinach to the boiling water for 10 seconds and drain thoroughly, squeezing out any excess water.

Arrange the drained spinach in your serving bowls along with the cooked king prawns and a pinch of bonito flakes, then slowly pour in your dashi soup. Serve immediately.

KING PRAWNS ON TOAST

An old-style, restaurant-worthy classic in less than 10 minutes! Impress your guests with whole king prawns lavishly loaded onto, crispy fried toast and served with your favourite dipping sauce.

5 MINUTES   **3 MINUTES**   **SERVES 4**

500ml (2 cups) vegetable oil
100g (3½oz/about 8) raw king prawns (jumbo shrimp), peeled and deveined
1 egg, beaten
pinch of salt
pinch of white pepper
1 tbsp cornflour (cornstarch)
4 slices of thick sliced white bread, crusts removed and sliced in half
3 tbsp dipping sauce of your choice

Pour the oil into a saucepan and heat to 180°C (350°F). If you don't have a thermometer, you can test the oil by dropping a piece of bread into the oil; if the oil is hot enough the bread should sizzle and float.

Carefully slice the king prawns lengthways along their back and gently flatten out to form a butterfly shape. Place into a bowl with the egg, salt, pepper and cornflour (cornstarch) and gently massage the ingredients together. Lay the trimmed slices of bread on a worktop and place a flattened king prawn onto each slice, pressing down gently; this will help it to stick.

Once the oil is hot enough, carefully place the king prawn bread slices into the oil (you may need to cook in a couple of batches). Fry for 2–3 minutes; the bread will naturally tip prawn-side down so you may need to gently poke the slices with a pair of chopsticks to submerge them enough to gain a golden colour on the underside. Once the prawns are cooked all the way through and the toast is golden, remove from the oil, drain on kitchen paper and serve hot with your favourite dipping sauce.

MUNG BEAN NOODLE & VEGETABLE SOUP

Don't be put off by a slightly longer list of ingredients – in just a few short minutes you'll be dropping them all into the pan together and simmering your way to soupy deliciousness!

5 MINUTES   **5 MINUTES**   **SERVES 2**

vegan

1.2 litres (5 cups) vegetable stock
2 tbsp Chinese rice wine
  (Shaoxing wine)
½ tbsp light soy sauce
1 tsp paprika or mild chilli powder
1 tsp Chinese five spice
100g (3½oz) pre-fried or marinated
  tofu pieces
60g (½ cup) sliced carrot
  (about ½ large carrot)
1 courgette (zucchini), halved
  lengthways and then sliced
  into half-moons
60g (1 cup) sliced mushrooms
100g (2 cups) beansprouts
  (canned or fresh)
thumb-sized piece of ginger,
  peeled and sliced
50g (1¾oz) dried mung bean
  (glass) noodles (about 1 nest)
¼ iceberg lettuce, shredded
salt, to taste
white pepper, to taste
1 tsp sesame oil

Pour the vegetable stock into a large saucepan and add the rice wine, soy sauce, spices, tofu, vegetables and ginger. Bring to the boil and simmer for 2 minutes.

Add the nest of noodles to the pan and after around 3–5 minutes add your lettuce. Season to taste with salt and pepper, then ladle into serving bowls and finish with a drizzle of sesame oil.

Kwoklyn's tip
Shave minutes off your preparation time by using pre-sliced carrots, mushrooms, courgettes and lettuce.

LAKSA CURRY SOUP

Laksa curry soup is a fusion of Chinese, Malay and Indonesian influences, thought to have originated from as early as the sixteenth century when Chinese sailors made berth at the coastal settlements of Indonesia.

2 MINUTES

5 MINUTES

SERVES 2

vegan

1 tbsp vegetable oil
2 tbsp laksa paste (use your favourite brand)
1 x 400ml (14fl oz) can coconut milk
180–200g (3–4 cups) beansprouts
150g (5oz) marinated tofu pieces
80g (3oz) ready-to-wok thin rice noodles
1 tsp chopped fresh chilli
2 tsp light soy sauce
3 spring onions (scallions), thinly sliced
2 wedges of lime

Place your wok over a medium-high heat. Add the oil and laksa paste and fry for 1–2 minutes.

Add the coconut milk and bring to the boil, then add the beansprouts and marinated tofu pieces. Bring it all back to the boil and simmer for 1 minute.

Add the ready-to-wok rice noodles and chopped chilli and simmer for a further minute. Taste and adjust your seasoning using the light soy sauce. Transfer to bowls, sprinkle with spring onions (scallions) and serve with a wedge of lime.

PORK & GREEN BEAN SOUP

With the smooth umami of the dashi stock and the gentle heat of the ginger and white pepper, this soup is perfect for those cold grey days when all you want is a simple bowl of hearty warmth.

5 MINUTES **5 MINUTES** **SERVES 2**

1 litre (4 cups) dashi stock
2 tsp ginger purée
2 tsp light soy sauce
100g (3½oz) pork fillet,
  cut into thin slices
8 green beans, cut into
  2cm (¾in) lengths
100g (3½oz) soft tofu,
  cut into 2cm (¾in) cubes
pinch of salt
pinch of white pepper
3 spring onions (scallions),
  thinly sliced on the diagonal

Pour the dashi stock, ginger purée and soy sauce into a saucepan and gently bring to the boil.

At the same time, bring another saucepan of water to the boil, then add the sliced pork and green beans and simmer for 2–3 minutes until cooked, then drain.

Arrange the cooked pork and green beans in two bowls, along with the cubed soft tofu. Season the dashi soup to taste with salt and white pepper, then slowly pour over the pork, tofu and beans. Garnish with spring onion (scallion) slices and serve immediately.

TOFU & SWEETCORN SOUP

An amped-up twist on the popular sweetcorn soup, packed with bite-sized veggies and smooth creamy tofu pieces.

3 MINUTES   **5 MINUTES**   **SERVES 4**

vegan

1.2 litres (5 cups) vegetable stock
1 tbsp Chinese rice wine
  (Shaoxing wine)
2 tsp light soy sauce
1 tsp sugar
100g (3½oz) carrot batons,
  chopped in half
150g (5oz) canned straw
  mushrooms, cut in half
1 x 425g (15oz) can creamed
  sweetcorn
100g (⅔ cup) frozen sweetcorn
150g (3½oz) frozen diced tomato
  (use fresh if prepared)
80g (⅔ cup) frozen petits pois
2 tbsp cornflour (cornstarch)
  mixed with 4 tbsp water
200g (7oz) soft tofu, cut into
  2cm (¾in) cubes
2 tsp sesame oil
salt and white pepper, to taste

Pour the stock, rice wine and light soy sauce into a saucepan, add the sugar, carrots, straw mushrooms and sweetcorn (canned and frozen) and bring to the boil. Once boiling, add the diced tomato and petits pois and bring the soup back to the boil.

Give the cornflour (cornstarch) mixture a good stir and gently pour into the soup to thicken to the consistency of single (light) cream. Once thickened turn off the heat, add salt and white pepper to taste and then gently stir in the cubed tofu. Transfer to serving bowls and drizzle over the sesame oil.

RICE NOODLE SOUP WITH CHICKEN & MUSHROOM

This dish conjures up images of customers sitting outside *dai pai dongs* (open air food stalls) on the streets of Hong Kong: heads down to the bowl, slurping the thick noodles that are impossible to catch with chopstick or spoon, unceremoniously sweating from the heat of the soup and the added spice of the chilli.

3 MINUTES   **7 MINUTES**   **SERVES 2**

150g (5oz) dried flat rice noodles
150g (5oz) chicken breast, diced
150g (5oz) white mushrooms, sliced
1 litre (4 cups) chicken stock
½ tsp dark soy sauce
1 tsp light soy sauce
½ tsp chilli powder (optional)
½ tsp garlic powder (optional)
pinch of white pepper
3 spring onions (scallions), diced
salt, to taste
drizzle of sesame oil

Bring a saucepan of water to the boil, add the flat rice noodles and cook for 2 minutes until soft, then drain and leave to one side.

While your noodles are boiling, place the remaining ingredients (except for the spring onions/scallions, salt and sesame oil) into a saucepan and bring to the boil, then turn down to a simmer. Using a pair of scissors roughly chop your softened rice noodles into 8cm (3in) pieces and add to your soup.

After 5 minutes check the soup for seasoning and season to taste with salt. Transfer to serving bowls, sprinkle with spring onions and a drizzle of sesame oil and serve immediately.

SPICY PEPPER OMELETTE

This provides quick satisfaction for those mornings when hunger pangs cry out and you need more than just a bowl of cereal!

3 MINUTES   **5-6 MINUTES**   **SERVES 2**

vegetarian

5 eggs
pinch of salt
pinch of white pepper
pinch of paprika
2 tbsp water
½ tsp muscovado sugar
½ tsp cornflour (cornstarch)
2 tbsp vegetable oil
100g (⅔ cup) diced onion
150g (1 cup) diced mixed
   (bell) peppers
1 tsp diced chilli

Whisk the eggs, salt, pepper, paprika, water, sugar and cornflour (cornstarch) together in a bowl until frothy.

Place your wok over a medium-high heat, add the oil and fry the onion, peppers and chilli for 2–3 minutes until golden brown. Give your egg mixture another quick whisk and then pour over the onion mixture and turn the heat down to medium-low. Once the bottom is brown and the top is beginning to set, carefully flip the omelette over and cook for a further minute. Transfer to a serving plate and enjoy.

TAIWANESE-STYLE OMELETTE WITH GRAVY

Inspired by the late-night snacks often found at Taiwanese night markets, this substantial omelette drizzled in rich Chinese gravy is sure to satisfy!

5 MINUTES   **4–5 MINUTES**   **SERVES 2**

3 eggs, beaten
125ml (½ cup) water
2 tbsp sweet potato starch
  (see Kwoklyn's tip)
pinch of salt
pinch of white pepper
100g (2 cups) beansprouts
150g (5oz) cooked prawns (shrimp)
150g (5oz) chopped cooked ham
2 spring onions (scallions),
  thinly sliced on the diagonal
250ml (1 cup) chicken stock
½ tbsp cornflour (cornstarch)
1 tsp sugar
1 tbsp oyster sauce
1 tsp dark soy sauce
1 tbsp vegetable oil

Combine the eggs, water, sweet potato starch, salt, pepper, beansprouts, prawns (shrimp), ham and half the chopped spring onions (scallions) together in a bowl.

Add the chicken stock, cornflour (cornstarch), sugar, oyster sauce and dark soy sauce to a saucepan and stir to combine. Place the saucepan over a medium heat and gently bring to the boil. Once thickened, turn off the heat and leave to one side.

Heat a non-stick wok over a medium-high heat, then add the oil; once hot pour in the egg mixture and allow it to cook on one side for 2–3 minutes before flipping over on to the other side. Once both sides are cooked, fold the omelette in half, transfer to a serving plate, pour over the gravy and sprinkle with the remaining spring onions.

Kwoklyn's tip
Sweet potato starch can be found in Asian supermarkets, online, or in some health food shops.

VEGETABLES

BROCCOLI & CAULIFLOWER IN MUSHROOM SAUCE

Raise the profile of your vegetable side dishes with a velvety smooth mushroom sauce and just a hint of deliciously pungent Chinese rice wine.

2 MINUTES   **8 MINUTES**   **SERVES 2**

vegan

375–400g (13–14oz) broccoli
    and cauliflower florets
150g (5oz) carrot batons
200g (7oz) baby corn, halved
    lengthways (or use canned
    baby corn)
250ml (1 cup) vegetable stock
3 tbsp mushroom stir-fry sauce
1 tbsp Chinese rice wine
    (Shaoxing wine)
1 tsp sugar
1 tsp cornflour (cornstarch)
1 tsp sesame oil

Bring a large saucepan of salted water to the boil, add the broccoli, cauliflower and carrots and blanch for 3–5 minutes until tender, adding the baby corn for the last 2 minutes. Drain and arrange on your serving plate.

Mix the stock, mushroom stir-fry sauce, rice wine, sugar, cornflour (cornstarch) and sesame oil together in a wok and bring to the boil. Once boiling and thickened, pour over your blanched vegetables and serve.

CHINESE BROCCOLI & OYSTER SAUCE

This succulent Chinese vegetable is also known as 'gai lan'; bright green in colour, it's packed with nutrients and is a great source of vitamin E. It's very popular in China, especially when paired with the distinct rich umami flavour of oyster sauce.

2 MINUTES　　　**8 MINUTES**　　　**SERVES 2**

450g (1lb) Chinese broccoli (gai lan)
1 tsp salt
3 tbsp oyster sauce
1 tbsp vegetable oil
1 tsp sesame oil

Trim the Chinese broccoli (gai lan) by removing any hard stems or yellow leaves, then cut into 15cm (6in) strips.

Bring a large saucepan of water to the boil, add the salt and blanch the broccoli for 4–5 minutes until tender. Drain and arrange on a serving plate.

Mix the oyster sauce, vegetable oil and sesame oil together in a bowl and drizzle over the Chinese broccoli. Serve immediately.

CHINESE-STYLE BUFFALO FLORETS

Enjoyed by vegetarians and meat eaters alike, these crispy-coated tender florets smothered in tangy, spicy buffalo sauce will be a stampede on your taste buds!

3 MINUTES   **7 MINUTES**   **SERVES 2**

vegetarian

1 egg
200–300g (7–10oz) cauliflower
 florets
25g (¼ cup) cornflour (cornstarch)
250ml (1 cup) vegetable oil
2 tbsp fermented chilli bean paste
 (doubanjiang)
5 tbsp rice vinegar or
 apple cider vinegar
1½ tbsp tomato purée (paste)
2 tbsp light soy sauce
2 tbsp sugar

Whisk the egg in a large bowl. Add the cauliflower florets to the bowl and mix well.

Lightly coat the cauliflower florets with the cornflour (cornstarch) and bang off any excess.

Heat the oil in a wok over a high heat and fry the cornflour-coated florets for 3–4 minutes, turning regularly to ensure even cooking and browning. Remove the cooked cauliflower to a plate and carefully tip the excess oil from the wok into a heatproof bowl to use for another recipe (once cool, strain to remove any residue).

Return the cauliflower to the wok, place over a high heat and add the chilli bean paste (doubanjiang), vinegar, tomato purée (paste), soy sauce and sugar. Stir well and cook for a minute or two until just starting to bubble and the sugar has dissolved. Transfer to a plate and enjoy. Serve any excess sauce alongside the florets for dipping.

Kwoklyn's tip
Re-use the excess oil to cook Crispy Chilli Tofu (page 37) or Green Beans in Black Bean Sauce (page 41).

CRISPY CHILLI TOFU, BAMBOO SHOOTS & WATER CHESTNUTS

Lightly fried tofu pieces and crunchy vegetables all lusciously wrapped in the unmistakeable aroma of my dad's favourite sauce, doubanjiang.

2 MINUTES   **8 MINUTES**   **SERVES 2**

vegan

225g (8oz) firm tofu, cut
  into 2cm (¾in) cubes
2 tbsp hoisin sauce
50g (½ cup) cornflour (cornstarch)
250ml (1 cup) vegetable oil
1 x 227g (8oz) can sliced bamboo
  shoots, drained
1 x 227g (8oz) can sliced water
  chestnuts, drained
2 tsp garlic purée
1 tbsp sugar
2 tbsp fermented chilli bean paste
  (doubanjiang)
½ tbsp rice vinegar
125ml (½ cup) water
1 tbsp toasted sesame seeds

Coat the tofu cubes in the hoisin sauce, then lightly dust with cornflour (cornstarch) and bang off any excess.

Heat the oil in a wok over a high heat and fry the tofu pieces for 3 minutes, turning regularly to ensure even cooking and browning. Using a slotted spoon, remove the tofu and drain on kitchen paper, then carefully tip the excess oil from the wok into a heatproof bowl to use for another recipe (once cool, strain to remove any residue).

Place the wok back over a high heat, add the bamboo shoots, water chestnuts and garlic purée and stir-fry for 1–2 minutes. Add the sugar, fermented chilli bean paste (doubanjiang), rice vinegar and water and continue to cook for a further 2 minutes. Once the sauce is bubbling and the sugar has dissolved, turn off the heat and drop in the drained tofu, tossing to coat. Transfer to a serving plate, sprinkle with the toasted sesame seeds and enjoy.

EIGHT TREASURE TOFU

In China, *ba* (eight) is a lucky number because it sounds like *fa*, which means wealth or fortune. This dish, with the eight vegetable treasures it holds, is considered to represent wealth and prosperity in all its many forms.

3 MINUTES   **5 MINUTES**   **SERVES 2**

vegan

2 tbsp vegetable oil
150g (1 cup) diced onion
3 celery sticks, cut into 3cm (1in) pieces on the diagonal
100g (1½ cups) sliced mushrooms
80g (½ cup) canned water chestnuts, drained and sliced
80g (½ cup) canned bamboo shoots, drained
80g (½ cup) sliced carrots
175–200g (6–7oz) marinated tofu cubes
80g (½ cup) salted peanuts

For the sauce
2 tbsp fermented chilli bean paste (doubanjiang)
1 tbsp Chinese rice wine (Shaoxing wine)
2 tsp sugar
1 tsp dark soy sauce
2 tbsp water
pinch of salt
pinch of white pepper
1 tsp cornflour (cornstarch)

Put all the ingredients for the sauce into a bowl and mix until well combined; leave to one side.

Place your wok over a medium-high heat; when hot add the oil followed by the onion and celery and stir-fry for 1 minute. Add the mushrooms and continue to stir-fry for another minute, then add the water chestnuts, bamboo shoots and carrots and stir-fry for another minute before adding the marinated tofu pieces.

Give the sauce mixture a quick stir and add to the wok. Once all of your ingredients are piping hot, add the peanuts, give everything a good mix and then transfer to your serving plate. Enjoy it as it is or with a bowl of steaming rice.

DEEP-FRIED GREEN BEANS IN BLACK BEAN SAUCE

Fresh green beans and fermented black beans come together in a simple recipe that makes this humble vegetable side dish anything but bland.

3 MINUTES   **5 MINUTES**   **SERVES 2**

vegan

250ml (1 cup) vegetable oil
450g (1lb) fine green beans, trimmed
5 spring onions (scallions), cut into
  5cm (2in) slices
2 tsp garlic purée
2 tsp ginger purée
1 tsp chilli flakes
1 tsp sesame oil

For the sauce
3 tbsp black bean and garlic sauce
  (see Kwoklyn's tip)
1 tbsp Chinese rice wine
  (Shaoxing wine)
60ml (¼ cup) vegetable stock
pinch of white pepper
½ tsp sugar
½ tsp cornflour (cornstarch)

Combine the ingredients for the sauce together in a bowl and mix well; leave to one side.

Heat the vegetable oil in a wok over a high heat and fry the green beans for 2 minutes, turning regularly to ensure even cooking. Using a slotted spoon or tongs, remove the green beans to a side dish and carefully tip the excess oil from the wok into a heatproof bowl to use for another recipe.

Return the green beans to the wok and place over a high heat, then add the spring onions (scallions), garlic and ginger purées and chilli flakes and fry for a few seconds until fragrant. Give the sauce mixture a stir and add to the wok, then bring to the boil and cook for a further minute to allow the sauce to thicken. Transfer to a serving plate, drizzle with sesame oil and enjoy.

Kwoklyn's tip
Black bean and garlic sauce can be found in Asian supermarkets, online, or in some larger supermarkets.

DICED MUSHROOMS WITH WALNUTS

Shiitake mushrooms were traditionally harvested from the mountain forests where they grew wild, but thanks to the ever-growing popularity of East Asian cuisines, they are now widely cultivated and readily available in most large supermarkets.

3 MINUTES   **5 MINUTES**   **SERVES 2**

vegan

1 tbsp vegetable oil
150g (1 cup) diced onion
2 tsp garlic purée
150g (5oz) chestnut mushrooms,
    cut into bite-sized pieces
100g (3½oz) diced carrot
1 x 150g (5oz) can shiitake
    (poku) mushrooms, cut
    into bite-sized pieces
1 x 227g (8oz) can straw mushrooms
60g (½ cup) walnuts
drizzle of sesame oil

For the sauce
125ml (½ cup) vegetable stock
1 tbsp Chinese rice wine
    (Shaoxing wine)
½ tbsp rice vinegar
1 tsp light soy sauce
1 tsp dark soy sauce
1 tsp sugar
pinch of white pepper
½ tsp cornflour (cornstarch)

Combine the ingredients for the sauce together in a bowl and mix well. Set to one side.

Place a wok over a medium-high heat; when hot add the vegetable oil followed by the diced onion and the garlic purée, fry for 1 minute. Add the chestnut mushrooms and stir-fry for a further 1 minute, then add the carrot and shiitake (poku) and straw mushrooms.

After another minute of cooking, add the walnuts, then give your sauce a quick stir and add to the wok. Bring to the boil, stirring continuously, and continue to cook until the sauce has thickened. Transfer to a plate and drizzle with sesame oil before serving.

CHINESE MIXED VEGETABLES

Serve as a side dish to your main meal or pile on top of freshly steamed jasmine rice and let the sauce run deep for a sumptuous bowl of vegetable goodness.

3 MINUTES   **5 MINUTES**   **SERVES 4**

vegan

2 tbsp vegetable oil
100g (¾ cup) sliced onion
2 tsp garlic purée
2 tsp ginger purée
350g (12oz) trimmed
   tenderstem broccoli
150g (5oz) sugarsnap peas
1 x 227g (8oz) can bamboo shoots
100g (⅔ cup) sliced carrots
250g (9oz) pak choi (bok choy),
   cut into bite-sized pieces
1 x 227g (8oz) can straw mushrooms
pinch of salt
pinch of white pepper
pinch of sugar
drizzle of sesame oil

For the sauce
2 tbsp mushroom stir-fry sauce
½ tbsp dark soy sauce
250ml (1 cup) vegetable stock
2 tsp cornflour (cornstarch)

Mix the ingredients for the sauce in a bowl until well combined and set to one side.

Heat a wok over a medium-high heat, then add the vegetable oil, onion and garlic and ginger purées and fry for 1 minute. Add the broccoli and sugarsnap peas and stir-fry for 30 seconds before adding the bamboo shoots, carrots, pak choi (bok choy) and straw mushrooms along with the salt, white pepper and sugar.

Give your sauce a quick mix before adding to the wok, then bring to the boil, mixing the whole time. Continue to cook until your sauce has thickened. Transfer to a serving plate and drizzle with sesame oil.

GENERAL TSO'S CHILLI TOFU

Named after Zuo Zongtang, a Qing Dynasty statesman and military leader, this dish is comfort food 101. Perfect for those who like spicy food, but are trying to cut down on their meat intake.

4 MINUTES   **6 MINUTES**   **SERVES 2**

vegan

1 tbsp vegetable oil
200g (7oz) cubed tofu pieces
1 bunch of spring onions (scallions),
   cut into 5cm (2in) slices
5 dried red chillies
1 tsp garlic purée
1 tbsp toasted sesame seeds

For the sauce

1 tsp cornflour (cornstarch)
2 tbsp Chinese rice wine
   (Shaoxing wine)
2 tbsp sugar
1 tbsp rice vinegar
2 tbsp fermented chilli bean paste
   (doubanjiang)
3 tbsp light soy sauce

Combine all the ingredients for the sauce in a bowl, mix well and set to one side.

Place your wok over a medium-high heat; when hot and add the oil and then the tofu pieces and fry for 1–2 minutes. Add the spring onion (scallions), dried chillies and garlic purée and fry for a further minute.

Give your sauce a quick mix, add to the wok and bring to the boil, stirring the whole time. Continue to cook for a further 2 minutes, allowing the sauce to thicken. Transfer to a serving plate and sprinkle with the toasted sesame seeds. Enjoy it as it is or with noodles.

SPICY MUSHROOMS

In their many shapes and sizes, mushrooms aren't always the prettiest vegetable on the shelf; however, they are deliciously versatile with their uniquely earthy flavours and are also bursting with essential vitamins.

5 MINUTES   **5 MINUTES**   **SERVES 2**

vegan

1 tbsp vegetable oil
2 tsp garlic purée
2 tsp ginger purée
250g (9oz) closed cap
   mushrooms, sliced
1 x 150g (5oz) can shiitake
   (poku) mushrooms, drained
   and sliced
1 x 227g (8oz) can straw mushrooms
drizzle of sesame oil
60g (½ cup) walnuts, crumbled
   but not crushed

For the sauce
60ml (¼ cup) vegetable stock
2 tbsp fermented chilli bean paste
   (doubanjiang)
1 tbsp Chinese rice wine
   (Shaoxing wine)
1 tsp dark soy sauce
1 tsp sugar
pinch of white pepper
½ tsp cornflour (cornstarch)

Mix all the sauce ingredients together in a bowl until well combined and then set to one side.

Place your wok over a medium-high heat; when hot add the vegetable oil, then the garlic and ginger purées and fry for a few seconds until fragrant. Add the sliced closed cap mushrooms and stir-fry for a further 1 minute, then add the shiitake (poku) and straw mushrooms and fry for another minute.

Give your sauce a quick stir and add it to the wok. Bring the sauce to the boil, mixing the whole time, and continue to cook until the sauce has thickened. Transfer to a plate, drizzle with sesame oil and sprinkle with crumbled walnuts before serving.

MARINATED TOFU WITH CHINESE MUSHROOMS

Estimates suggest that the origin of shiitake mushrooms can be traced as far back as the Cretaceous period, over 100 million years ago. That's some seriously old fungus!

4 MINUTES   **6 MINUTES**   **SERVES 2**

vegan

1 tbsp vegetable oil
5 spring onions (scallions),
   cut into 5cm (2in) slices
1 tsp ginger purée
1 tsp garlic purée
3 celery sticks, cut into batons
100g (3½oz) carrot batons
1 x 284g (10oz) can shiitake
   (poku) mushrooms, drained and
   cut into bite-sized pieces
175–200g (6–7oz) marinated tofu
drizzle of sesame oil

For the sauce
125ml (½ cup) vegetable stock
1 tbsp Chinese rice wine
   (Shaoxing wine)
1 tbsp mushroom stir-fry sauce
1 tsp sugar
pinch of white pepper
½ tsp cornflour (cornstarch)

Put all the ingredients for the sauce into a bowl and mix until well combined. Set to one side.

Place your wok over a medium-high heat; when hot add the vegetable oil, then the spring onion (scallions) and ginger and garlic purées and stir-fry for 1 minute. Add the celery and carrots and stir-fry for another minute. Finally, stir in the shiitake (poku) mushrooms and tofu.

Give your sauce a quick stir and add to the wok, then bring to the boil, mixing the whole time. Continue to cook until the sauce has thickened. Transfer to a serving plate and drizzle with sesame oil.

SPICY TOFU WITH COURGETTES

Spicy nuggets of tofu tossed together with soft bites of courgette and shiitake mushrooms, crisp water chestnuts and crunchy carrots, all lusciously enrobed in a rich chilli-spiced sauce.

3 MINUTES   **7 MINUTES**   **SERVES 2**

vegan

2 tbsp vegetable oil
150g (1 cup) diced onion
1 tsp ginger purée
5 courgettes (zucchini), halved
    lengthways and then cut into
    half-moons
1 x 150g (5oz) can shiitake
    (poku) mushrooms, drained
    and cut into bite-sized pieces
100g (⅔ cup) canned sliced
    water chestnuts
80g (⅔ cup) sliced carrots
1 tsp chilli flakes
200g (7oz) spicy tofu cubes
    (you can use marinated too)
1 tsp sesame oil

For the sauce

1 tbsp Chinese rice wine
    (Shaoxing wine)
125ml (½ cup) vegetable stock
2 tbsp Sriracha chilli sauce
1 tsp sugar
½ tsp cornflour (cornstarch)
pinch of white pepper
1 tsp light soy sauce
½ tsp dark soy sauce

Put all the sauce ingredients into a bowl and mix well. Leave to one side.

Place your wok over a medium-high heat; when hot add the vegetable oil, then the diced onion and ginger purée and fry for 1 minute. Add the courgettes (zucchini) and fry for another minute, then add the shiitake (poku) mushrooms, water chestnuts, carrots, chilli flakes and tofu, and continue to stir-fry for another 2 minutes.

Give the sauce a quick stir and add to the wok. Bring the sauce to the boil and cook for a further minute or two, allowing the sauce to thicken. Transfer to a serving plate and drizzle with sesame oil.

STIR-FRIED BROCCOLI & CAULIFLOWER WITH HOISIN SAUCE

Tender chunks of broccoli and cauliflower in a sweet aromatic hoisin sauce.

2 MINUTES   **8 MINUTES**   **SERVES 2**

vegan

450g (1lb) broccoli and
   cauliflower florets
2 tbsp hoisin sauce
2 tbsp Chinese rice wine
   (Shaoxing wine)
60ml (¼ cup) vegetable stock
½ tsp cornflour (cornstarch)
1 tbsp vegetable oil
2 tsp garlic purée
1 tsp sesame oil

Bring a large saucepan of salted water to the boil, add the broccoli and cauliflower florets and blanch for 4–5 minutes until tender. Drain and set aside.

While the veg is cooking, combine the hoisin sauce, rice wine, stock and cornflour (cornstarch) together in a bowl and set to one side.

Place your wok over a medium-high heat, add the (vegetable) oil and garlic purée and stir-fry for a few seconds until fragrant, then add the drained broccoli and cauliflower florets and fry for a further minute.

Give the sauce a quick stir and add to the wok. Bring to the boil and continue to cook until the sauce has thickened. Transfer to a serving plate and drizzle with sesame oil.

STIR-FRIED SPINACH

This delicately aromatic wilted spinach is dressed in a sweet soy sauce and can be ready in minutes.

2 MINUTES   **4 MINUTES**   **SERVES 2**

vegan

1 tbsp light soy sauce
1 tbsp dark soy sauce
1 tsp sugar, plus an extra
   pinch for seasoning
1 tbsp vegetable oil
2 tsp garlic purée
1 tsp ginger purée
450g (1lb) fresh washed spinach
pinch of salt
drizzle of sesame oil

Combine the light and dark soy sauces and sugar together in a bowl and mix well. Set to one side.

Place your wok over a medium–high heat, then add the vegetable oil along with the garlic and ginger purées and fry for a few seconds until fragrant. Add the spinach and continue to stir-fry until wilted, then add a pinch each of salt and sugar and mix well.

Tip any excess water out of the wok, then arrange the cooked spinach on a serving plate. Finally drizzle over your soy sauce mixture followed by the sesame oil.

TOFU WITH CHILLI PLUM SAUCE

Sweet and spicy is the order of the day! Heap on top of freshly steamed rice or toss into some springy noodles for a speedy midweek supper that will have your taste buds tingling.

3 MINUTES   **7 MINUTES**   **SERVES 2**

vegan

1 tbsp vegetable oil
200g (7oz) cubed firm tofu
1 bunch of spring onions (scallions), cut into 5cm (2in) slices; reserve some for serving
2 tsp ginger purée
2 tsp garlic purée
150g (1 cup) diced onion
150g (1 cup) sliced (bell) peppers
250g (4 cups) sliced mushrooms
170ml (scant ¾ cup) plum sauce
60ml (¼ cup) water
1 tbsp chilli paste (avoid using pastes that are 'pickled' in white wine vinegar, as it affects the final flavour of the dish)

Place your wok over a medium–high heat; once hot add the oil, then the tofu pieces and fry for 1 minute.

Add the spring onions (scallions) and ginger and garlic purées and fry for a further minute. Now add the onion, peppers and mushrooms and cook for another 2 minutes.

Finally stir in the plum sauce, water and chilli paste and bring to the boil. Cook for a further 2 minutes, allowing the sauce to reduce and thicken slightly. Transfer to a serving plate, sprinkle with the reserved spring onions and enjoy.

Kwoklyn's tip
Make your sauce hotter or milder to suit your own taste preference by adding a little more or less of the chilli paste.

SEAFOOD

BOOZY SCALLOPS
WITH WATER SPINACH

These tender scallops are stir-fried with sherry and rich green Chinese water spinach, called *hin choy* in Cantonese.

4 MINUTES   **6 MINUTES**   **SERVES 2**

300g (10oz) Chinese water spinach
1 tbsp vegetable oil
300g (10oz) scallops, sliced
  horizontally into 2 discs
1 tsp ginger purée
150ml (generous ½ cup)
  vegetable stock
1 tbsp oyster sauce
2 tbsp dark soy sauce
3 tbsp Chinese rice wine
  (Shaoxing wine) or sherry
1 tsp cornflour (cornstarch)
  mixed with 2 tsp water
1 tsp sesame oil

Rinse the spinach in cold water and drain, separating the white stalks from the leaves.

Heat a non-stick wok over a medium–high heat, add the vegetable oil and gently fry the scallop slices for 1 minute, turning once during cooking, then remove from the wok to rest.

Place the wok back over the heat, add the white spinach stalks and ginger purée and stir-fry for 1 minute, then add the spinach leaves along with the stock, oyster sauce and soy sauce. Once boiling, return the scallops to the wok and add the rice or sherry wine.

Give the cornflour (cornstarch) mixture a stir to loosen and gradually drizzle into the wok, stirring gently and continuously to thicken the sauce. Turn off the heat, transfer to a serving plate and finish with a drizzle of sesame oil.

CHILLI KING PRAWNS

These spicy king prawns are delicious with your favourite rice and noodle dishes, or if you're feeling the flair for fusion, why not load them on top of a hunk of lavishly buttered sourdough toast?

3 MINUTES   **7 MINUTES**   **SERVES 2**

½ tbsp salt
½ tbsp Chinese five spice
1 tsp ground black pepper
250ml (1 cup) vegetable oil
300g (10oz) raw king prawns (jumbo shrimp), peeled and deveined
2 tsp garlic purée
150g (1 cup) diced onion
150g (1 cup) diced mixed (bell) peppers (fresh or frozen)
2 tsp chopped red chillies
1 tsp sesame oil

Combine the salt, five spice and black pepper together in a bowl, mix well and set to one side.

Heat the vegetable oil in a non-stick wok over a high heat, add the king prawns (jumbo shrimp) and cook for 2–3 minutes, stirring regularly to ensure even cooking. Transfer the king prawns to a plate to rest and carefully tip any excess oil from the wok into a heatproof bowl to use in another recipe.

Place the wok back over a high heat, add the garlic purée, onions, peppers and chillies and stir-fry for 2 minutes. Add the cooked king prawns back into the wok and toss everything together.

Sprinkle in the dry seasonings, tossing or mixing the ingredients to ensure everything is evenly coated. Transfer to a serving plate and drizzle with sesame oil.

Kwoklyn's tip
Re-use the excess oil to cook Fried Fish in Cantonese-style Chilli Sauce (page 66). You might want to keep the excess oil that you've used to cook the seafood separately from any oil that you plan to use for meat and vegetable dishes, as the oil can hold on to the flavour of the fish.

CHINESE FISH CAKES & BROCCOLI

These springy fish cakes are served with bitter-sweet Chinese broccoli in a sumptuous sauce, rich with the taste of the sea.

3 MINUTES　　**6 MINUTES**　　**SERVES 2**

300g (10oz) Chinese broccoli (gai lan)
250–300g (9–10oz) Chinese fish cakes (or use fish balls, see Kwoklyn's tip)
1 tbsp vegetable oil
2 tsp garlic purée
drizzle of sesame oil

For the sauce
60ml (¼ cup) chicken stock
1 tbsp oyster sauce
½ tbsp light soy sauce
1 tbsp Chinese rice wine (Shaoxing wine)
2 tsp sugar
pinch of white pepper
½ tsp cornflour (cornstarch)

Trim the Chinese broccoli, removing any hard stems or yellow leaves, then cut into 10cm (4in) strips. Chop the fish cakes (or fish balls) into bite-sized pieces.

Combine the sauce ingredients in a bowl, mix well and set to one side.

Place a wok over a medium-high heat, add the vegetable oil and garlic purée and fry for a few seconds until fragrant. Next add the chopped fish cakes and fry for 1 minute, stirring throughout for even cooking, followed by the Chinese broccoli. Cook for a further 2 minutes.

Give your sauce a stir and add to the wok, then bring to the boil. Continue to cook for a further 1–2 minutes, allowing the sauce to thicken. Transfer to serving plate and finish with a drizzle of sesame oil.

Kwoklyn's tip
Chinese fish cakes or fish balls are available from the chilled or freezer section of Asian supermarkets or online. They are pre-cooked and will heat in the pan from frozen; though, if you have time, defrosting them first and then chopping them is easy and will reduce the overall cooking time.

CRAYFISH TAILS WITH CUCUMBER

A smaller, freshwater relation to lobster, these sweetly succulent crayfish tails will deliver a simple taste of luxury to your meal.

4 MINUTES **6 MINUTES** **SERVES 2**

1 tbsp vegetable oil
5 spring onions (scallions),
   cut into 5cm (2in) slices
2 tsp garlic purée
2 tsp ginger purée
1 tsp dried chilli flakes
1 large cucumber, deseeded
   and cut into 5cm (2in) strips
200g (7oz) cooked crayfish tails (or
   use king prawns/jumbo shrimp)
drizzle of sesame oil

For the sauce
60ml (¼ cup) chicken stock
1 tbsp oyster sauce
½ tbsp light soy sauce
1 tbsp Chinese rice wine
   (Shaoxing wine)
2 tsp sugar
½ tsp cornflour (cornstarch)

Combine the ingredients for the sauce together in a bowl, mix well and set to one side.

Place a wok over a medium-high heat, add the vegetable oil and fry the spring onions (scallions), garlic and ginger purées and chilli flakes for 1 minute, stirring throughout for even cooking. Add the cucumber strips and cook for a further 2–3 minutes.

Give your sauce a stir and add to the wok. Bring to the boil and then add the crayfish tails. Continue to cook for a further minute, allowing the sauce to thicken. Remove from the heat, transfer to a serving plate and finish with a drizzle of sesame oil. Enjoy these as they are or with a tasty bowl of noodles.

DEEP-FRIED SICHUAN KING PRAWNS

No-fuss succulent king prawns, spiked with a generous dusting of tongue-tingling Sichuan peppercorns.

3 MINUTES   **7 MINUTES**   **SERVES 2**

1½ tsp salt
1 tsp ground Sichuan peppercorns
½ tsp Chinese five spice
350g (12oz) whole raw king prawns (jumbo shrimp) in their shells
250ml (1 cup) vegetable oil
5 garlic cloves, finely chopped or grated
5 spring onions (scallions), cut into 2cm (¾in) diagonal pieces

Combine the salt, ground Sichuan peppercorns and five spice in a bowl and set to one side.

Heat the oil in a wok over a medium-high heat and fry the king prawns (jumbo shrimp) for 3–4 minutes, stirring throughout for even cooking. Transfer to a wire rack or a plate lined with kitchen paper and carefully pour any excess oil from the wok into a heatproof bowl to use in another recipe.

Return the cooked king prawns to the wok along with the garlic and spring onions (scallions) and cook for 1 minute over a medium heat, stirring continuously. Finally, sprinkle in your seasoning mix and toss to ensure every prawn is coated. Transfer to a serving plate and tuck in.

FRIED FISH IN CANTONESE-STYLE CHILLI SAUCE

These delicate cubes of white fish are wrapped in a tangy sweet chilli sauce – perfect with a bowl of egg fried rice or a side of fries and an ice-cold beer!

3 MINUTES **7 MINUTES** **SERVES 2**

1 tsp salt
50g (½ cup) cornflour (cornstarch)
300–350g (10–12oz) diced white fish
  (use your favourite)
250ml (1 cup) vegetable oil
1 tbsp ginger purée
2 tbsp garlic purée
2 spring onions (scallions), thinly
  sliced on the diagonal

For the sauce
4 tbsp tomato ketchup
4 tbsp sweet chilli sauce
2 tbsp Chinese rice wine
  (Shaoxing wine)
1 tbsp light soy sauce
1 tbsp sugar

Combine all the ingredients for the sauce together in a bowl, mix well and set to one side.

In another bowl mix together the salt and cornflour (cornstarch) and use to lightly coat the fish pieces, banging off any excess.

Heat the oil in a wok over a high heat and fry the coated fish pieces for 3–4 minutes, stirring regularly to ensure even cooking and browning. Transfer the fish to a wire rack or plate lined with kitchen paper and carefully pour any excess oil from the wok into a heatproof bowl to use in another recipe (once cool, strain to remove any residue).

Place the wok back over a low-medium heat, add the ginger and garlic purées and fry for 30 seconds until fragrant. Give your sauce mixture a stir, add it to the wok and bring to the boil. Cook for a further 2 minutes to allow the sauce to thicken, then turn off the heat and gently place the cooked fish into the sauce, carefully stirring to coat each piece. Transfer to your serving plate and garnish with the spring onions.

KING PRAWN, SWEET GINGER & PINEAPPLE

A tangy take on the classic sweet and sour with juicy chunks of pineapple and a delicate fragrance from the sweet, pickled ginger.

3 MINUTES   **7 MINUTES**   **SERVES 2**

1 tbsp vegetable oil
300g (10oz) raw king prawns (jumbo shrimp), peeled and deveined
1 tsp garlic purée
150g (1 cup) diced onion
80g (3oz) pickled ginger
1 x 230g (8oz) can pineapple chunks, drained
150g (1 cup) sliced carrots

For the sauce
250ml (1 cup) chicken stock
2 tsp cornflour (cornstarch)
½ tbsp tomato purée (paste)
1 tbsp tomato ketchup
1 tbsp sugar
2 tbsp Chinese rice wine (Shaoxing wine)

Combine the ingredients for the sauce together in a bowl. Mix well and set to one side.

Heat your wok over a medium-high heat, add the oil and prawns (jumbo shrimp) and stir-fry for 1 minute, then add the garlic purée and fry for a further 30 seconds. Next add the diced onion, pickled ginger, pineapple and carrots and fry for a further 2 minutes.

Give the sauce a quick stir and add to your wok. Bring to the boil, mixing the whole time, and continue to cook for a further 2 minutes, allowing the sauce to thicken. Transfer to a serving plate and enjoy.

DEEP-FRIED KING PRAWNS WITH GREEN BEANS

An all-round sweetly savoury dish with the juiciness of the king prawns and the crunch of the green beans being carefully retained through fast cooking.

3 MINUTES　　**7 MINUTES**　　**SERVES 2**

250ml (1 cup) vegetable oil
300g (10oz) raw king prawns (jumbo shrimp), peeled and deveined
200g (7oz) fine green beans, trimmed
2 tsp garlic purée
2 tsp ginger purée
1 tsp sesame oil

For the sauce
2 tbsp yellow bean sauce
1 tbsp hoisin sauce
1 tbsp Chinese rice wine (Shaoxing wine)
60ml (¼ cup) vegetable stock
½ tsp sugar
½ tsp cornflour (cornstarch)

Combine the sauce ingredients together in a bowl, mix well and set to one side.

Heat the vegetable oil in a wok over a high heat and fry the king prawns (jumbo shrimp) and green beans for 3 minutes, stirring regularly to ensure even cooking. Transfer the king prawns and green beans to a wire rack or a plate lined with kitchen paper and carefully tip any excess oil from the wok into a heatproof bowl to use in another recipe.

Return the king prawns and green beans to the wok, add the garlic and ginger purées and fry for a few seconds over a high heat until fragrant.

Give the sauce a stir and add to the wok, then bring to the boil. Cook for a further minute, allowing the sauce to thicken, then transfer to a serving plate and drizzle with sesame oil.

Kwoklyn's tip
Re-use the excess oil to cook Fried Fish in Cantonese-style Chilli Sauce (page 66). You might want to keep the excess oil that you've used to cook the seafood separately from any oil that you plan to use for meat and vegetable dishes, as the oil can hold on to the flavour of the fish.

GREEN BEANS WITH FISH FLAKES

These tender green beans are infused with the rich umami flavours of China and Japan.

2 MINUTES   **5 MINUTES**   **SERVES 2**

500ml (2 cups) dashi stock
(see Kwoklyn's tip)
1 tbsp light soy sauce
2 tbsp Chinese rice wine
(Shaoxing wine)
250g (9oz) green beans, trimmed
and cut into 5cm (2in) slices
pinch of bonito fish flakes

Add the dashi stock, soy sauce and rice wine to a saucepan along with the trimmed green beans and gently bring to the boil.

Cook the beans for about 4 minutes; once they are tender, remove from the pan with a slotted spoon, reserving the cooking liquor. Place the drained beans on a serving plate, sprinkle with the bonito fish flakes and pour over a little of the reserved cooking liquor.

Kwoklyn's tip
Dashi stock and bonito fish flakes are available to buy in Asian supermarkets or online.

FRIED SQUID WITH PURPLE SPROUTING BROCCOLI

With the sweet and tangy taste of the rice wine increasing your appetite, you're sure to be coming back for more of this delicious dish!

3 MINUTES   **7 MINUTES**   **SERVES 2**

1 tbsp vegetable oil
300g (10oz) fresh squid, sliced into bite-sized pieces and scored (your fishmonger will do this for you)
2 tsp ginger purée
3 celery sticks, cut into 3cm (1in) pieces on the diagonal
225g (8oz) purple sprouting broccoli
250ml (1 cup) chicken or fish stock
2 tbsp oyster sauce
½ tbsp dark soy sauce
½ tbsp sugar
pinch of salt
pinch of white pepper
2 tbsp Chinese rice wine (Shaoxing wine)
1 tbsp cornflour (cornstarch) mixed with 2 tbsp water
drizzle of sesame oil

Place your wok over a medium-high heat, add the vegetable oil and fry the squid for 1 minute, stirring throughout for even cooking. Add the ginger purée and fry for a further 20 seconds, then add the celery and broccoli and continue to cook for a further 2 minutes.

Add the stock along with the oyster sauce, soy sauce, sugar, salt and pepper and bring to the boil, then stir in the rice wine. Give the cornflour (cornstarch) mix a quick stir to loosen and slowly add to the sauce, mixing continuously until the sauce is thick enough to coat the back of a spoon.

Remove from the heat, transfer to a serving plate and finish with a drizzle of sesame oil.

HONG KONG CURRY FISH BALLS

Made famous by the street hawkers of Hong Kong, these golden fried fish balls, skewered and dipped in curry sauce, were sold from wooden snack trolleys.

1 MINUTE   **7 MINUTES**   **SERVES 2**

250ml (1 cup) vegetable oil
200–250g (7–9oz) fish balls
 (defrosted if frozen), see Kwoklyn's
 tip on page 61
5 tbsp Chinese or Japanese
 curry sauce mix
500ml (2 cups) warm water
2 spring onion (scallion) greens,
 roughly chopped on the diagonal

Heat the oil in a wok over a high heat and fry the fish balls for 2–3 minutes, stirring regularly to ensure even cooking and browning. Remove the cooked fish balls and place on a wire rack or plate lined with kitchen paper and set aside.

Combine the curry sauce mix and water in a saucepan and slowly bring up to a simmer. Add the fried fish balls and cook for a further 3 minutes over a low heat. Check the consistency of your sauce: if it is too thick, add a little more water; if it is too thin, simply simmer until you reach the desired consistency. Transfer to a serving plate, sprinkle with spring onion (scallion) greens and eat while hot. Enjoy the fish balls on their own or piled on top of a nice bowl of rice.

KING PRAWN IN XO SAUCE

A relatively new and yet iconic Chinese condiment, XO sauce was developed in Hong Kong in the 1980s for Cantonese cuisine; it's now considered by many to be a staple ingredient in southern Chinese cooking.

3 MINUTES   **7 MINUTES**   **SERVES 2**

1 tbsp vegetable oil
300g (10oz) raw king prawns (jumbo shrimp), peeled and deveined
5 spring onions (scallions), cut into 5cm (2in) slices
180g (6oz) mangetout (snowpeas)
60ml (¼ cup) chicken or fish stock
3 tbsp XO sauce
1 tbsp Chinese rice wine (Shaoxing wine)

Place your wok over a medium-high heat, add the oil and fry the king prawns (jumbo shrimp) for 2 minutes, stirring throughout for even cooking.

Add the spring onions (scallions) and cook for 30 seconds, then add the mangetout (snowpeas) and continue to stir-fry for a further 2 minutes before adding the stock and the XO sauce. Give everything a good mix, then add the rice wine and stir through to fully combine with the other sauce ingredients. Remove from the heat and transfer to a serving plate.

KING PRAWN, FRESH GINGER & CELERY

Juicy king prawns are accompanied by a medley of crisp vegetable bites and smothered in a smooth rich sauce.

4 MINUTES   **6 MINUTES**   **SERVES 2**

1 tbsp vegetable oil

300g (10oz) raw king prawns (jumbo shrimp), peeled and deveined

5cm (2in) cube of ginger, peeled and cut into thin slices

1 tsp garlic purée

5 celery sticks, cut into 3cm (1in) pieces on the diagonal

1 x 227g (8oz) can sliced bamboo shoots, drained

1 x 227g (8oz) can sliced water chestnuts, drained

250ml (1 cup) chicken or fish stock

2 tbsp oyster sauce

½ tbsp dark soy sauce

½ tbsp sugar

pinch of salt

pinch of white pepper

3 tbsp Chinese rice wine (Shaoxing wine)

1 tbsp cornflour (cornstarch) mixed with 2 tbsp water

drizzle of sesame oil

Place your wok over a medium-high heat, add the vegetable oil and fry the king prawns (jumbo shrimp) for 1 minute, stirring throughout for even cooking. Add the ginger slices and garlic purée and stir-fry for a further 20 seconds, then add the celery, bamboo shoots and water chestnuts. Continue to cook for a further minute.

Add the stock along with the oyster sauce, soy sauce, sugar, salt and pepper and give it all a good stir to combine. Once it has come to the boil, add the rice wine, then give the cornflour (cornstarch) mixture a quick stir to loosen and slowly add to the sauce, mixing continuously until the sauce is just thick enough to coat the back of the spoon.

Remove from the heat and transfer to a serving plate. Finish with a drizzle of sesame oil.

KING PRAWN WITH MIXED VEG & CASHEWS

Crispy veggies and juicy king prawns in a sweet yellow bean sauce, all topped off with a handful of creamy, crunchy cashew nuts.

3 MINUTES   **7 MINUTES**   **SERVES 2**

1 tbsp vegetable oil
150g (1 cup) diced onion
2 tsp garlic purée
2 tsp ginger purée
1 tsp dried chilli flakes
80g (½ cup) canned sliced
　water chestnuts
80g (½ cup) canned sliced
　bamboo shoots
80g (½ cup) sliced carrots
120g (4oz) cauliflower florets
200g (7oz) cooked king prawns
　(jumbo shrimp)
50g (½ cup) roasted cashew nuts

For the sauce
125ml (½ cup) fish stock (or you
　can use vegetable or chicken)
1½ tbsp yellow bean sauce
1 tbsp Chinese rice wine
　(Shaoxing wine)
2 tsp sugar
½ tsp cornflour (cornstarch)

Combine the ingredients for the sauce together in a bowl, mix well and set to one side.

Place your wok over a medium-high heat, add the oil and fry the diced onion with the garlic and ginger purées and chilli flakes for 1 minute, stirring throughout for even cooking.

Next add the water chestnuts, bamboo shoots, carrots and cauliflower florets and stir-fry for a further 2–3 minutes. Give the sauce a quick stir, add to the wok and bring to the boil, then add the cooked prawns (jumbo shrimp). Continue to cook for a further minute to allow the sauce to thicken. Remove from the heat, transfer to a serving plate and sprinkle with the roasted cashew nuts.

SAUTÉED SCALLOPS WITH MANGETOUT

With their melt-in-the-mouth, buttery texture, these scallops are sure to be the king or queen of your 10-minute banquet!

2 MINUTES　　**8 MINUTES**　　**SERVES 2**

1 tbsp vegetable oil
300g (10oz) scallops
100g (⅔ cup) diced onion
2 tsp ginger purée
1 tsp garlic purée
200g (7oz) tenderstem broccoli
100g (⅔ cup) sliced carrots
200g (7oz) mangetout (snowpeas)
1 tsp sesame oil

For the sauce
250ml (1 cup) vegetable stock
2 tbsp Chinese rice wine
　(Shaoxing wine) or sherry
½ tbsp dark soy sauce
1 tbsp oyster sauce
pinch of white pepper
1 tsp cornflour (cornstarch)

Combine the ingredients for the sauce in a bowl, mix well and leave to one side.

Heat a non-stick wok over a medium-high heat, add the vegetable oil and gently fry the scallops for 2–3 minutes, turning once during cooking. Remove from the wok as soon as you are happy that the scallops are cooked and set aside on a plate to rest.

Place the wok back over the heat, add the diced onion and ginger and garlic purées and fry for 1 minute. Next add the broccoli and sliced carrot and stir-fry for 45 seconds.

Give your sauce a quick stir and add to the wok along with the mangetout (snowpeas). Bring it all to the boil and allow to cook for a further 1–2 minutes until the sauce has thickened to your desired consistency.

Turn off the heat and return the cooked scallops to the wok. Give everything a final toss and transfer to a serving plate, finished off with a drizzle of sesame oil.

Kwoklyn's tip
Scallops can quickly become chewy if overcooked. Keep your pan hot and turn them quickly halfway through to ensure even cooking.

FRIED FISH, GARLIC, GINGER & SPRING ONION

In this delicious dish, lightly coated chunks of fish are seasoned with the holy trinity of Cantonese cooking: garlic, ginger and spring onion.

3 MINUTES　　**7 MINUTES**　　**SERVES 2**

1 tsp salt, plus an extra pinch
　for seasoning
50g (½ cup) cornflour (cornstarch)
300–350g (10–12oz) diced white
　fish, defrosted if frozen (use your
　favourite)
250ml (1 cup) vegetable oil
6cm (2½in) cube of ginger, peeled
　and cut into slices
1 bunch of spring onions (scallions),
　cut into 5cm (2in) slices
3 garlic cloves, roughly sliced
pinch of white pepper
2 tbsp Chinese rice wine
　(Shaoxing wine)
drizzle of sesame oil

In a large bowl mix together the salt and cornflour (cornstarch) and use to lightly coat the fish pieces, banging off any excess.

Heat the vegetable oil in a wok over a high heat and fry the coated fish pieces for 3–4 minutes, stirring regularly to ensure even cooking and browning. Transfer the fish to a wire rack or plate lined with kitchen paper and carefully pour any excess oil from the wok into a heatproof bowl to use in another recipe (once cool, strain to remove any cornflour residue).

Place the wok back over a low-medium heat, add the ginger, spring onions (scallions) and garlic and fry for 30–45 seconds until fragrant, then return the fried fish to the wok. Season with a pinch of salt and white pepper followed by the rice wine. Make sure you toss the fish carefully at this stage as you don't want it to break up in the wok. Transfer to a serving plate and finish with a drizzle of sesame oil.

Kwoklyn's tip
Re-use the excess oil to cook Fried Fish in Cantonese-style Chilli Sauce (page 66) or Deep-fried King Prawns with Green Beans (page 68). You might want to keep the excess oil that you've used to cook the seafood separately from any oil that you plan to use for meat and vegetable dishes, as the oil can hold on to the flavour of the fish.

SWEET CHILLI SALMON LETTUCE WRAPS

Forget floppy, stodgy sandwiches! Impress your lunch date with these 'build your own' wraps – cool crisp lettuce filled with sticky, spicy salmon flakes and fresh cucumber.

4 MINUTES   **6 MINUTES**   **SERVES 2**

1 tbsp vegetable oil
2 thin salmon steaks
pinch of salt
pinch of white pepper
4 tbsp sweet chilli sauce, plus extra
  to serve
4 whole iceberg lettuce leaves
3 spring onions (scallions),
  sliced into thin rings
¼ cucumber, cut into
  half-moon slices

Heat the oil in a non-stick frying pan over a medium-high heat. Place the salmon steaks into the pan skin-side down, season with a pinch of salt and pepper and allow to fry for 3 minutes. Turn the salmon steaks over and season again with salt and pepper, frying again for a further 2 minutes. Turn the salmon steaks once more, drizzle each steak with 2 tablespoons of the sweet chilli sauce and fry for another minute.

Transfer to a serving plate and start to build your wraps: break the salmon, including the crispy skin, into chunks and sprinkle half a fillet into each lettuce leaf along with a pinch of spring onion (scallions), a few slices of cucumber and another generous drizzle of sweet chilli sauce. Gently wrap the leaf around the filling, head down and tuck in.

Kwoklyn's tip
The best way to separate iceberg lettuce leaves while keeping them intact is to hold the head of lettuce under a slowly running cold tap, as the leaves fill with water they should start to peel away from the head without breaking. Gently ease them free and pat dry with kitchen paper.

MEAT

BEEF & ONION WITH MIXED PEPPERS

This is Cantonese cooking perfection, from the rich aromatic umami sauce and the tender beef fillet, right through to the little bit of background heat from the ground black pepper. A true Cantonese classic!

4 MINUTES   **6 MINUTES**   **SERVES 2**

2 tbsp vegetable oil
200g (1½ cups) sliced onion
200g (1½ cups) sliced mixed
  (bell) peppers
300g (10oz) beef fillet,
  cut into very thin slices
2 tsp garlic purée
2 tsp ginger purée
1 tsp ground black pepper

For the sauce
250ml (1 cup) chicken stock
1 tbsp Chinese rice wine
  (Shaoxing wine)
1 tbsp oyster sauce
2 tsp cornflour (cornstarch)

Combine the sauce ingredients in a bowl, mix well and set to one side.

Place your wok over a medium-high heat, add the oil and stir-fry the onions and peppers for 3 minutes. Next add the beef with the garlic and ginger purées and stir-fry for a further 30 seconds.

Give the sauce mixture a quick stir and pour into your wok, bringing it to the boil and continuing to cook for another minute, or until the sauce has thickened to your preferred consistency.

Turn off the heat and add the black pepper, then give it all a good mix and transfer to a serving plate. This dish also works well when served with rice on the side.

BEEF & MUSHROOM CURRY

A firm favourite in many households, this classic Chinese takeaway curry with tender slivers of beef and juicy mushrooms is guaranteed to satisfy those cravings.

3 MINUTES   **7 MINUTES**   **SERVES 2**

500ml (2 cups) warm water
5 tbsp Chinese or Japanese
  curry sauce mix
2 tbsp vegetable oil
150g (1 cup) sliced onion
200g (7oz) mushrooms, sliced
300g (10oz) beef fillet, cut into
  very thin slices
2 tsp garlic purée
pinch of salt
pinch of sugar

Combine the water and curry sauce mix in a saucepan and slowly bring up to a simmer. If your sauce is too thick, add a little more water; if it is too thin, simmer until you reach your desired consistency.

While the sauce is simmering, place a non-stick wok over a medium-high heat, add the oil and fry the sliced onion for 1 minute, then add the sliced mushrooms and continue to fry for a further 2 minutes. Next add the beef with the garlic purée, a pinch of salt and a pinch of sugar and fry for a further 30 seconds.

Give the curry sauce a quick stir, pour into your wok, and bring it to the boil. Continue to cook for another minute. Check the consistency of your sauce: if it is too thick, add a little more water; if it is too thin, simply simmer until you reach the desired consistency. Turn off the heat and transfer to a serving plate. Enjoy as it is or serve with rice.

BEEF, SPRING ONION & CASHEWS

A delicious combination of garlic, ginger and spring onion with the Indonesian influence of spicy satay.

4 MINUTES **6 MINUTES** **SERVES 2**

1 tbsp vegetable oil
300g (10oz) beef fillet,
    cut into very thin slices
2 tsp garlic purée
2 tsp ginger purée
1 bunch of spring onions (scallions),
    cut into 5cm (2in) slices
drizzle of sesame oil
80g (⅔ cup) salted cashew nuts

For the sauce
125ml (½ cup) chicken stock
½ tbsp satay paste
1 tsp cornflour (cornstarch)

Combine the sauce ingredients in a bowl, mix well and set to one side.

Place a wok over a medium-high heat, add the vegetable oil and fry the beef for 30 seconds, then add the garlic and ginger purées and fry for a further 30 seconds. Next add the spring onions (scallions) and continue to stir-fry for 1–2 minutes.

Give the sauce mixture a quick stir and pour into your wok, bringing it to the boil and continuing to cook for another minute, or until the sauce has thickened to your preferred consistency.

Transfer to a serving plate, drizzle with sesame oil and scatter the cashew nuts over the top.

BLACK PEPPER BEEF WITH MIXED GREEN VEGETABLES

Believed to have origins in the Fujian province of China, the combination of thinly sliced beef seasoned with an ample dose of black pepper has been a classic Chinese-American favourite since the 1940s. The classic Black Pepper Beef dish would typically always use green peppers; here I've also used mangetout and fine green beans for extra crunch.

4 MINUTES　　**6 MINUTES**　　**SERVES 2**

1 tbsp vegetable oil
300g (10oz) beef fillet,
　cut into very thin slices
2 tsp garlic purée
75g (½ cup) sliced mixed (bell)
　peppers
150g (5oz) mangetout (snowpeas)
150g (5oz) fine green beans
2 tsp ground black pepper
drizzle of sesame oil

For the sauce
125ml (½ cup) chicken stock
2 tbsp oyster sauce
1 tbsp Chinese rice wine
　(Shaoxing wine)
1 tsp light soy sauce
1 tsp cornflour (cornstarch)

Combine the sauce ingredients in a bowl, mix well and set to one side.

Place a wok over a medium-high heat, add the vegetable oil and fry the beef for 30 seconds, then add the garlic purée and fry for a further 30 seconds. Next add the mixed (bell) peppers, mangetout (snowpeas) and fine green beans and continue to stir-fry for 1–2 minutes; the vegetables should still be tender and crisp.

Give the sauce mixture a quick stir and pour into your wok. Bring it all to the boil and continue to cook for another minute, or until the sauce has thickened to your preferred consistency. Turn off the heat, add the black pepper and give it all a final stir. Transfer to a serving plate and drizzle with sesame oil.

CANTON LAMB & ONIONS

According to traditional Chinese medicine, lamb is an excellent meat for warding off the cold and keeping warm, making this a perfect mid-winter choice.

3 MINUTES　　**7 MINUTES**　　**SERVES 2**

350g (12oz) lamb fillet,
　cut into thin slices
1 tsp sugar
½ tsp salt
1 tsp ground black pepper
1 tbsp light soy sauce
1 tsp dark soy sauce
2 tsp cornflour (cornstarch)
2 tbsp vegetable oil
1 tsp garlic purée
1 tsp ginger purée
300g (2 cups) sliced onion
drizzle of sesame oil

Place the lamb, sugar, salt, black pepper, light and dark soy sauces and cornflour (cornstarch) in a bowl and give everything a good mix, ensuring the lamb is evenly coated. Set to one side.

Place a wok over a medium-high heat, add the vegetable oil and fry the garlic and ginger purées for 10 seconds until fragrant, then add the sliced onion and stir-fry for 2 minutes until translucent and slightly coloured at the edges.

Add the marinated lamb and continue to stir-fry for a further 3 minutes until cooked all the way through. Finally add 2–3 tablespoons water and mix well to create a sauce. Transfer to a serving plate and finish with a drizzle of sesame oil. Enjoy this dish as it is or serve with rice on the side.

BEEF FILLET WITH BEANSPROUTS

Many years ago, before the fast-growing popularity of these crispy, juicy sprouts made them readily available in the UK, my mum grew mung bean sprouts in an old bathtub to keep up with the demand of my dad's first Chinese restaurant.

4 MINUTES   **6 MINUTES**   **SERVES 2**

1 tbsp vegetable oil
300g (10oz) beef fillet,
   cut into very thin slices
2 tsp garlic purée
1 bunch of spring onions (scallions),
   cut into 5cm (2in) slices
200g (4 cups) beansprouts
drizzle of sesame oil

For the sauce
250ml (1 cup) chicken stock
1 tbsp oyster sauce
2 tbsp Chinese rice wine
   (Shaoxing wine)
1 tsp cornflour (cornstarch)

Combine the sauce ingredients in a bowl, mix well and set to one side.

Place a wok over a medium-high heat, add the vegetable oil and fry the beef for 30 seconds, then add the garlic purée and fry for a further 30 seconds. Next add the spring onions (scallions) and beansprouts and continue to stir-fry for 1–2 minutes.

Give the sauce a quick stir and pour into the wok, bringing it all to the boil and continuing to cook for a further minute, or until the sauce has thickened to your preferred consistency. Transfer to a serving plate and drizzle with sesame oil.

MINCED BEEF & TOMATO

This dish makes use of the truly versatile minced beef, loaded with chunky fresh tomatoes and carrying the distinct aroma of Chinese rice wine.

3 MINUTES   **7 MINUTES**   **SERVES 2**

1 tbsp vegetable oil
100g (⅔ cup) diced onion
  (fresh or frozen)
1 tsp garlic purée
250g (9oz) minced (ground) beef
1 tbsp soy sauce
1 tbsp Chinese rice wine
  (Shaoxing wine)
1 x 400g (14oz) can chopped
  tomatoes
3 tbsp tomato ketchup
1 tbsp tomato purée (paste)
125ml (½ cup) chicken stock
1 tsp salt
1 tsp sugar
1 tbsp cornflour (cornstarch),
  mixed with 2 tbsp water

Heat the oil in a non-stick wok over a medium–high heat. Add the onion and garlic purée and fry for 1–2 minutes, then add the minced (ground) beef and fry for around 3 minutes until browned, using the back of your spoon to break down any lumps.

Add the remaining ingredients, except the cornflour (cornstarch) mixture, and continue to cook. Once the ingredients are bubbling away, slowly add the cornflour mixture, stirring all the time. Turn off the heat and serve over steamed rice.

Kwoklyn's tip
The cornflour and water mixture will set slightly while waiting to be used but you can simply give it another mix to loosen again before adding to your dish.

MINUTE STEAK CANTON

These thin pieces of tender steak cook in minutes and are then smothered in a rich, aromatic, tangy, Canton-style sauce.

2 MINUTES   **8 MINUTES**   **SERVES 2**

1 tbsp vegetable oil
350–400g (12–14oz) thin-cut steak
pinch of salt
pinch of white pepper
150g (1 cup) sliced onion
½ tsp Chinese five spice
½ tsp cornflour (cornstarch)
125ml (½ cup) tomato ketchup
3 tbsp brown sauce
2 tbsp Worcestershire sauce
3 tbsp sugar
1 tbsp Chinese rice wine
  (Shaoxing wine)
60ml (¼ cup) water

Heat a non-stick frying pan over a medium-high heat and add the oil. Season the steak on both sides with a small pinch of salt and white pepper and then fry the steak for 1–2 minutes on each side, or until cooked to your liking. Transfer the steak to a side plate and allow to rest.

Add the sliced onion to the same frying pan and fry for 1 minute, then add the Chinese five spice and fry for a further minute, mixing well.

Add the cornflour (cornstarch) and mix well. Then add the remainder of the ingredients, except the steak, and bring to the boil. Continue cooking for a further 1–2 minutes to allow the sauce to thicken. Arrange the steak on a serving plate and pour over the sauce and onions.

MISO SAUCY PORK

Miso is naturally packed full of umami; when combined with tangy tomato ketchup and succulent pieces of pork this dish delivers with every single mouthful.

2 MINUTES   **8 MINUTES**   **SERVES 2**

1 egg
pinch of salt
350g (12oz) diced lean pork
250ml (1 cup) vegetable oil
2 spring onions (scallions),
  cut into thin diagonal strips

For the sauce
2 tsp cornflour (cornstarch)
125ml (½ cup) tomato ketchup
125ml (½ cup) dry red wine
1 tsp miso paste
1 tsp light soy sauce
pinch of white pepper

Combine the ingredients for the sauce in a bowl, mix well and set to one side.

Beat the egg and a pinch of salt in a large bowl, add the pork and massage the eggs into the meat.

Heat the oil in a wok over a high heat and fry the pork pieces for 4–5 minutes, stirring regularly to ensure even cooking and browning. Transfer the pork to a wire rack or a plate lined with kitchen paper, then carefully tip the excess oil from the wok into a heatproof bowl to use in another recipe (once cool, strain to remove any residue).

Return the pork to the wok over a high heat, give the sauce mixture a quick stir and add to the wok. Bring to the boil and cook for a further 2–3 minutes to allow the sauce to thicken. Once the pork is fully cooked through, transfer to a serving plate and garnish with the chopped spring onions (scallions).

Kwoklyn's tip
Re-use the excess oil to make Pork and Chillies (page 98).

PORK & CHILLIES

Not for the faint-hearted, this dish really brings the heat!

4 MINUTES   **6 MINUTES**   **SERVES 2**

250g (9oz) lean pork loin steak,
   cut into strips
pinch of salt
½ tsp sugar
1 tsp cornflour (cornstarch)
2 tsp sesame oil
½ tbsp light soy sauce
1 tsp dark soy sauce
250ml (1 cup) vegetable oil
2 tsp garlic purée
2 tsp ginger purée
100g (3½oz) fresh red bird's-eye
   chillies, stalks removed and cut
   into long strips
2 tbsp Chinese rice wine
   (Shaoxing wine)

Combine the pork, salt, sugar, cornflour (cornstarch), sesame oil and light and dark soy sauces in a bowl, mixing well to ensure the pork is evenly coated with all of the ingredients. Set to one side.

Heat the vegetable oil in a wok over a high heat and fry the pork pieces for 1–2 minutes, stirring regularly to ensure even cooking and browning. Transfer the pork to a wire rack or a plate lined with kitchen paper, then carefully tip the excess oil from the wok into a heatproof bowl to use in another recipe (once cool, strain to remove any residue).

Place the wok back over a high heat, add the garlic and ginger purées and give them a quick stir, then add the chopped chillies and fry for 1 minute. Return the fried pork strips to the wok, add the rice wine and give everything a quick stir. Serve immediately.

Kwoklyn's tip
Re-use the excess oil to make Miso Saucy Pork (page 97).

PORK CHAR SIU

When you're craving the rich taste of barbecued Cantonese roasted pork but time is against you, this dish is the perfect cheat to achieve all you desire.

4 MINUTES   **6 MINUTES**   **SERVES 2**

250g (9oz) lean pork loin steak, cut into strips
1 tbsp vegetable oil
1 tsp garlic purée
75g (½ cup) sliced onion
300g (6 cups) beansprouts
1 tsp sugar
pinch of white pepper
pinch of salt

For the marinade
1 tbsp oyster sauce
1 tsp sugar
1 tsp cornflour (cornstarch)

For the sauce
60ml (¼ cup) chicken stock
1 tbsp Chinese rice wine (Shaoxing wine)
3 tbsp char siu sauce
¼ tsp cornflour (cornstarch)

Place the pork into a bowl with all the marinade ingredients, give everything a good mix and set to one side.

In another bowl mix the sauce ingredients together and set to one side.

Place your wok over a high heat, add the oil and fry the pork pieces for 1–2 minutes, stirring regularly to ensure even cooking and browning. Add the garlic purée and, after a few seconds, add the sliced onion and fry for another minute. Add the beansprouts, sugar and a pinch of white pepper and salt.

Give the sauce mix a stir and add to the wok, then bring to the boil and cook for a further minute to allow the sauce to thicken. Transfer to a serving plate and enjoy.

RED CHILLI BEEF

So named for the many red ingredients that come together in perfect harmony in this dish, delivering mouthful after mouthful of sweet, tangy, fiery flavour.

 5 MINUTES   **5 MINUTES**   **SERVES 2**

300g (10oz) beef fillet,
   cut into very thin slices
1 tbsp paprika
2 tsp chilli powder
pinch of salt
2 tbsp vegetable oil
2 tsp garlic purée
5 celery sticks, cut into 2cm (¾in)
   diagonal slices
3 long red chillies, stalks removed,
   halved lengthways
3 spring onions (scallions), cut into
   2cm (¾in) diagonal slices
150g (5oz) cherry tomatoes, halved

For the sauce
125ml (½ cup) chicken stock
1 tbsp tomato purée (paste)
3 tbsp tomato ketchup
3 tbsp honey
1 tbsp rice vinegar
1 tsp Tabasco
½ tsp cornflour (cornstarch)

Combine the sliced beef, paprika, chilli powder and salt together in a bowl, give everything a good mix and set to one side to marinate while you prepare the rest of the ingredients.

Combine all the ingredients for the sauce in a bowl, mix well and set to one side.

Place a wok over a medium-high heat, add the oil and fry the garlic purée and celery for 1–2 minutes, then add the marinated beef, chillies and spring onions (scallions) and stir-fry for 45 seconds before adding the halved cherry tomatoes.

Give the sauce mix a good stir and add to the wok, stirring gently to combine and then bringing it all to the boil. Once the sauce has thickened, taste and adjust the seasoning, adding more salt if required. Remove from the heat and serve.

RICE WINE BEEF

Succulent beef fillet slices are served with wilted spinach and peppery beansprouts, all dressed in a richly aromatic sauce.

5 MINUTES   **5 MINUTES**   **SERVES 2**

1 tbsp vegetable oil
300g (10oz) beef fillet,
　cut into very thin slices
2 tsp ginger purée
180g (6oz) baby spinach
200g (4 cups) beansprouts
drizzle of sesame oil

For the sauce
3 tbsp Chinese rice wine
　(Shaoxing wine)
1 tbsp oyster sauce
½ tbsp light soy sauce
½ tbsp dark soy sauce
½ tbsp sugar
125ml (½ cup) chicken stock
pinch of white pepper
2 tsp cornflour (cornstarch)

Combine the ingredients for the sauce in a bowl, mix well and set to one side.

Place a wok over a medium-high heat, add the vegetable oil and fry the beef for 30 seconds, then add the ginger purée and fry for a further 30 seconds. Next add the spinach and beansprouts, continuing to stir-fry for 1–2 minutes.

Give the sauce mixture a quick stir and pour into the wok, bringing it all to the boil and continuing to cook for a further minute, or until the sauce has thickened to your preferred consistency. Transfer to a serving plate and drizzle with sesame oil.

SERIOUSLY SWEET & SOUR PORK

Pickled ginger and fresh mixed peppers bring a sweet crunch to the sauce accompanying these Hong Kong-style meaty morsels.

2 MINUTES   **8 MINUTES**   **SERVES 2**

50g (½ cup) cornflour (cornstarch)
½ tsp salt
350g (12oz) diced lean pork
250ml (1 cup) vegetable oil
150g (1 cup) sliced mixed (bell) peppers
50g (2oz) pickled ginger

For the sauce
250ml (1 cup) water
2 tsp cornflour (cornstarch)
1 tbsp tomato purée (paste)
2 tbsp tomato ketchup
3 tbsp rice vinegar (or use white wine vinegar or cider vinegar)
2 tbsp sugar

Combine the ingredients for the sauce in a bowl, mix well and set to one side.

Mix the cornflour (cornstarch) and salt together in a bowl, add the diced pork and give everything a good stir to ensure the pork is evenly coated.

Heat the oil in a wok over a high heat and fry the pork pieces for 4–5 minutes, stirring regularly to ensure even cooking and browning. Transfer the pork to a wire rack or a plate lined with kitchen paper, then carefully tip the excess oil from the wok into a heatproof bowl to use in another recipe (once cool, strain to remove any residue).

Return the pork to the wok over a high heat, add the mixed (bell) peppers and pickled ginger and fry for 1 minute. Give the sauce mixture a quick stir, add to the wok and bring to the boil; cook for a further 1–2 minutes to allow the sauce to thicken. Once the pork is fully cooked through, transfer to a serving plate. Serve the pork as it is or piled on top of rice.

SATAY LAMB STEAK WITH COCONUT RICE

Tender lamb steaks encrusted in spicy satay sauce, served on delicately flavoured coconut rice and tender green beans; rich and spicy meets smooth and fresh for a perfect balance of taste and texture in every bite.

3 MINUTES   **7 MINUTES**   **SERVES 2**

2 lean lamb leg steaks, about 225g (8oz) total weight
1 tbsp satay paste (use your favourite; I use Jimmy's Satay Sauce)
1 tbsp vegetable oil
150g (5oz) green beans (use frozen or fresh)
pinch of salt
1 x 250g (9oz) packet ready-cooked coconut rice

Put the kettle on. While the kettle is boiling, in a large bowl massage the lamb steaks with the satay paste and oil. Preheat a non-stick wok over a high heat.

Put the green beans into a saucepan with a pinch of salt, cover with boiling water and place over a medium-high heat. Meanwhile, add the marinated lamb steaks to the wok and cook for 2–3 minutes each side for medium, or until cooked to your liking.

While the lamb and beans are cooking, microwave the coconut rice following the packet instructions and transfer to serving bowls.

Drain the green beans and place over the rice, then top with the lamb steaks.

SPICY PORK WITH PEANUTS

Taking inspiration from the nutty spice of the much loved satay, whole peanuts bring a new level of creamy crunch to this dish.

4 MINUTES   **6 MINUTES**   **SERVES 2**

1 tbsp vegetable oil
250–300g (9–10oz) lean pork
   loin steak, cut into strips
   (or use stir-fry strips)
1 tsp garlic purée
1 tsp ginger purée
3 whole dried chillies,
   halved lengthways
80g (½ cup) unsalted peanuts
drizzle of sesame oil

For the sauce
60ml (¼ cup) chicken stock
1 tbsp Chinese rice wine
   (Shaoxing wine)
½ tbsp oyster sauce
1 tsp dark soy sauce
2 tsp sugar
½ tsp cornflour (cornstarch)
pinch of white pepper

Combine all the ingredients for the sauce in a bowl, mix well and set to one side.

Place a wok over a high heat, add the vegetable oil and fry the pork strips for 1–2 minutes, stirring regularly to ensure even cooking and browning. Next add the garlic and ginger purées, chillies and peanuts and stir-fry for 1 minute.

Give your sauce mix a stir and add to the wok, bringing it all to the boil and cooking for a further 1–2 minutes until the sauce has thickened. Transfer to a serving plate and drizzle with sesame oil. Serve the spicy pork as it is or with rice.

CHICKEN & DUCK

'BANG-BANG' CHICKEN SALAD

Traditionally served as a cold snack by the street vendors in China, the dish was named 'bang-bang' chicken because of the batons that were used to hammer the chicken to tenderize it.

10 MINUTES   **0 MINUTES**   **SERVES 2–4**

300g (10oz) cooked chicken breast, shredded (or you can use sliced chicken)
1 cucumber, cut into 5cm (2in) batons
150g (1 cup) grated carrot
3 spring onions (scallions), cut into 5cm (2in) slices

For the dressing
2 tbsp light soy sauce
1 tsp sugar
3 tbsp sweet chilli sauce
2 tbsp crunchy peanut butter
2 tsp toasted sesame seeds
1 tsp sesame oil
1–2 tbsp water

In a large bowl gently toss the cooked chicken, cucumber, grated carrot and spring onions (scallions). Transfer to a serving plate.

Combine all the ingredients for the dressing in a bowl; if your mixture is too thick, you can add a little more water. Once fully mixed and loose enough to pour, drizzle over your salad.

CHICKEN, BAMBOO SHOOTS & WATER CHESTNUTS

Tender pieces of chicken stir-fried with juicy bamboo shoots and crunchy water chestnuts in a rich Chinese gravy – this dish was very popular with the customers of my dad's Cantonese restaurant back in the late eighties and early nineties.

3 MINUTES   **7 MINUTES**   **SERVES 2**

1 tbsp vegetable oil
150g (1 cup) diced onion
150g (5oz) chicken breast, sliced
1 tsp garlic purée
80g (½ cup) sliced carrots
80g (½ cup) canned sliced
   bamboo shoots
80g (½ cup) canned sliced
   water chestnuts
½ tsp sugar
¼ tsp salt
pinch of white pepper
½ tbsp dark soy sauce
280ml (generous 1 cup)
   vegetable stock
1 tbsp Chinese rice wine
   (Shaoxing wine)
2 tbsp cornflour (cornstarch)
   mixed with 4 tbsp water
50g (½ cup) roasted salted
   cashew nuts

Heat your wok over a high heat and add the oil; once the wok begins to smoke, add the onion and fry for 1 minute. Next add the sliced chicken and cook for a further 2 minutes, or until the chicken starts to brown.

Add the garlic and cook for a further 30 seconds, then add the carrots, bamboo shoots, water chestnuts, sugar, salt, white pepper and dark soy sauce. Give everything a quick mix, add the stock and bring it all to the boil, then stir in the rice wine.

Give the cornflour (cornstarch) mixture a quick mix and slowly drizzle into the wok, stirring the ingredients at the same time, until you have the desired consistency; you may not need all of the cornflour mixture. The sauce should be thick enough to coat the ingredients but still pour. Transfer to a serving plate and finally garnish with the roasted cashew nuts.

Kwoklyn's tip
This dish can be cooked with chicken, beef, king prawns (jumbo shrimp), tofu or even your favourite vegetables, as the method is the same for each.

CHICKEN TERIYAKI

A popular dish from the menu of my street food bar, Wantons, these crispy chicken bites are served in a sweet sauce fusion of Japanese and Hawaiian origins.

2 MINUTES   **8 MINUTES**   **SERVES 2**

50g (½ cup) cornflour (cornstarch)
1 tsp salt
350g (12oz) diced chicken
  (breast or thigh)
250ml (1 cup) vegetable oil
150g (1 cup) diced onion
5 spring onions (scallions), roughly
  chopped on the diagonal
2 tsp garlic purée
2 tbsp Chinese rice wine
  (Shaoxing wine) or sake
2 tbsp light soy sauce
2 tbsp water
1 tbsp mirin
1 tbsp sugar

Mix the cornflour (cornstarch) and salt together in a bowl, then lightly coat the chicken pieces with the seasoned flour and bang off the excess.

Heat the oil in a wok over a high heat and fry the coated chicken pieces for 4–5 minutes, stirring regularly to ensure even cooking and browning. Transfer the chicken to a wire rack or a plate lined with kitchen paper, then carefully tip the excess oil from the wok into a heatproof bowl to use in another recipe (once cool, strain to remove any residue).

Return the chicken back to the wok over a high heat, add the diced onion, spring onions (scallions) and garlic purée and fry for a further 30 seconds. Add the remainder of the ingredients and continue to cook for a further 1–2 minutes. Serve and enjoy.

ROAST DUCK IN PLUM SAUCE

Originating from South China, Chinese plum sauce balances the richness of the roast duck with its harmonious blend of sweet, tart and spice flavours.

3 MINUTES **7 MINUTES** **SERVES 2**

250ml (1 cup) vegetable oil
breast from a whole deboned
    roasted Chinese duck (see
    Kwoklyn's tip)
1 tsp garlic purée
1 tsp ginger purée
1 x 230g (8oz) can pineapple chunks

For the sauce
3 tbsp plum sauce
1 tsp sugar
1 tbsp rice vinegar
2 tbsp water

Combine the ingredients for the sauce in a bowl, mix well and set to one side.

Place a non-stick wok over a medium-high heat, add the oil and fry the whole duck breast, turning regularly for even cooking, for 2–3 minutes until crispy and heated all the way through. Transfer the duck breast to a plate lined with kitchen paper, then tip any excess oil into a heatproof bowl to use in another recipe. Return the wok to a medium-high heat, add the garlic and ginger purées and fry for a few seconds until fragrant, then give your sauce mix a stir and add to your wok. Once the sauce comes to the boil, remove from the heat.

Carefully arrange the pineapple chunks on a serving plate, slice the duck breast into bite-sized pieces and arrange on top of the pineapple. Pour the sauce over the top and enjoy.

Kwoklyn's tip
Buy a whole deboned roasted Chinese duck from your local Asian supermarket and break it down into portions before storing in your freezer for use in other recipes.

CHILLI CHICKEN & SESAME SEEDS

Succulent chunks of chicken in a light crispy coating are tossed in a sweetly sticky chilli sauce and topped with a generous helping of nutty sesame seeds.

2 MINUTES   **8 MINUTES**   **SERVES 2**

50g (½ cup) cornflour (cornstarch)
½ tsp salt
250g (9oz) diced chicken
  (breast or thigh)
250ml (1 cup) vegetable oil
150g (1 cup) diced onion
3 tsp garlic purée
2 tsp ginger purée
3 tsp dried chilli flakes
5 spring onions (scallions), roughly
  chopped on the diagonal
2 tbsp toasted sesame seeds

For the sauce
4 tbsp rice vinegar
2 tbsp light soy sauce
4 tbsp honey

Mix the cornflour (cornstarch) and salt together in a bowl. Drop the chicken pieces into the bowl and lightly coat with the seasoned flour, banging off the excess.

Heat the oil in a wok over a high heat and fry the coated chicken pieces for 4–5 minutes, stirring regularly to ensure even cooking and browning. Meanwhile, combine the sauce ingredients in a bowl, mix well and set to one side.

Once the chicken is cooked, remove from the oil and place on a wire rack or plate lined with kitchen paper to drain while you carefully tip the excess oil from the wok into a heatproof bowl (you can use this in another recipe but strain once cool to remove any cornflour residue).

Place the wok back over a high heat, add the diced onion, garlic and ginger purées and chilli flakes and cook for 1 minute, then add the spring onions (scallions) and cook for a further 30 seconds.

Give your sauce mix a stir and add to the wok, bringing it all to a boil and allowing to reduce and thicken. Return the cooked chicken to the wok and toss to thoroughly coat in the sauce. Transfer to a serving plate and sprinkle generously with the toasted sesame seeds.

Kwoklyn's tip
Re-use the excess oil to make Garlic and Ginger Chicken (page 122) or Ginger and Lemon Chicken (page 124).

GARLIC & GINGER CHICKEN

Garlic ginger chicken is a simple and homely Chinese dish oozing with fresh aromatic flavours. With its rich, dark sauce it's great served over rice or noodles.

2 MINUTES   **8 MINUTES**   **SERVES 2**

50g (½ cup) cornflour (cornstarch)
½ tsp salt
250g (9oz) diced chicken
  (breast or thigh)
250ml (1 cup) vegetable oil
150g (1 cup) diced onion
5 garlic cloves, peeled and crushed
1 tsp garlic purée
1 tsp ginger purée
50g (2oz) pickled ginger
3 spring onions (scallions), roughly
  chopped on the diagonal

For the sauce
125ml (½ cup) chicken stock
1 tbsp light soy sauce
2 tsp rice vinegar
3 tbsp tomato ketchup
½ tbsp sugar
1 tsp cornflour (cornstarch)

Combine the ingredients for the sauce in a bowl, mix well and set to one side.

Mix the cornflour (cornstarch) and salt together in a large bowl, then add the chicken pieces and lightly coat with the seasoned flour, banging off the excess.

Heat the oil in a wok over a high heat and fry the chicken pieces for 4–5 minutes, stirring regularly to ensure even cooking and browning. Remove and drain the chicken on a wire rack or plate lined with kitchen paper and carefully tip the excess oil from the wok into a heatproof bowl to use in another recipe (once cool, strain to remove any residue).

Place the wok back over a high heat, add the diced onion, crushed garlic, garlic and ginger purées and pickled ginger and cook for 1 minute, then add half the spring onions (scallions) to cook for a further 30 seconds. Add the cooked chicken and mix well.

Give the sauce mix a quick stir and add to the wok, bring it all to the boil and stir continuously. Cook for a further 1 minute to allow the sauce to thicken, then transfer to a serving plate and garnish with the remaining spring onions.

Kwoklyn's tip
Re-use the excess oil to make Chilli Chicken and Sesame Seeds (page 121) or Ginger and Lemon Chicken (page 124).

GINGER & LEMON CHICKEN

Sticky sweet lemon-coated chicken pieces combined with a delicate background warmth of ginger makes this dish fresh and flavoursome.

---

3 MINUTES   **7 MINUTES**   **SERVES 2**

1 egg
½ tsp salt
250g (9oz) chicken breast,
   sliced into strips
250ml (1 cup) vegetable oil
100g (3½oz) pickled ginger
1 tsp ginger purée

For the sauce
60ml (¼ cup) lemon cordial
250ml (1 cup) water
2 tsp cornflour (cornstarch)
1 tbsp sugar

Combine the ingredients for the sauce in a bowl, mix well and set to one side.

Whisk the egg and salt together in a large bowl, add the chicken strips and massage the egg into the meat.

Heat the oil in a wok over a high heat and fry the coated chicken pieces for 3 minutes, stirring regularly to ensure even cooking and browning. Transfer the chicken to a wire rack or a plate lined with kitchen paper and carefully tip the excess oil from the wok into a heatproof bowl to use in another recipe.

Return the chicken to the wok over a high heat, add the pickled ginger and ginger purée and fry for 30 seconds. Give the sauce mix a stir, add to the wok and bring to the boil. Continue cooking for a further 2 minutes to allow the sauce to thicken, then transfer to a serving plate.

Kwoklyn's tip
Re-use the excess oil to make Chilli Chicken and Sesame Seeds (page 121) or Garlic and Ginger Chicken (page 122).

ROAST DUCK WITH PINEAPPLE

Duck has been roasted in China since the Southern and Northern dynasties period (AD 386–589) and roasted duck with pineapple is just one of the many delicious variations.

3 MINUTES **7 MINUTES** **SERVES 2**

1 tbsp vegetable oil
3 large slices of ginger
¼ whole deboned roasted
   Chinese duck, cut into slices
   (see Kwoklyn's tip)
75g (½ cup) diced onion
75g (½ cup) shredded carrot
2 spring onions (scallions), cut
   into 2cm (¾in) diagonal slices
1 x 230g (8oz) can pineapple
   chunks in syrup, drained
   (reserve the syrup)
salt, to taste

For the sauce
3 tbsp syrup from the
   canned pineapple
pinch of salt
1 tsp sugar
1½ tbsp rice vinegar
1 tbsp tomato ketchup
¼ tsp cornflour (cornstarch)

Combine the ingredients for the sauce in a bowl, mix well and set to one side.

Place a non-stick wok over a medium-high heat, add the oil and fry the ginger slices for a few seconds until fragrant. Add the duck slices and fry for 1 minute, stirring throughout for even cooking, then stir in the onion and carrot and cook for a further 2 minutes. Next add the spring onions (scallions) and after 30 seconds of stir-frying, put the pineapple in the wok.

Give the sauce mix a stir, add to the wok and bring to the boil. Continue to cook for a further 1–2 minutes to allow the sauce to thicken, then taste and adjust the seasoning by adding salt if required. Remove from the heat and transfer to a serving plate.

Kwoklyn's tip
Buy a whole deboned roasted Chinese duck from your local Asian supermarket and break it down into portions before storing in your freezer for use in other recipes.

GUNPOWDER CHICKEN

Often served at royal celebrations in China, conflicting stories abound as to whether Gunpowder Chicken was the creation of a Chinese alchemist or a chef who simply stumbled across this explosive combination of ingredients.

2 MINUTES   **8 MINUTES**   **SERVES 2**

2 tbsp vegetable oil
350g (12oz) chicken thigh fillets, diced
12 Thai red chillies, stalks removed and halved lengthways
1 tsp ground Sichuan peppercorns
1 bunch of spring onions (scallions), cut into 5cm (2in) slices
50g (⅓ cup) roasted peanuts

For the sauce
3 tbsp dark soy sauce
2 tbsp Chinese rice wine (Shaoxing wine)
2 tbsp Chinese black rice vinegar (Chinkiang)
125ml (½ cup) chicken stock
1 tbsp sugar
1 tsp cornflour (cornstarch)

Combine the ingredients for the sauce in a bowl, mix well and set to one side.

Heat the oil in a wok over a medium-high heat and fry the chicken for 3–4 minutes, stirring occasionally for even browning. Add the chillies and Sichuan peppercorns and fry for a further 1–2 minutes.

Give the sauce mix a stir and add to the wok, bringing it all to the boil and continuing to cook for a further 1–2 minutes to allow the sauce to thicken. Add the spring onions (scallions) and peanuts, give everything a good toss to combine and transfer to a serving plate. Serve the chicken as it is or with a nice bowl of noodles.

GINGER & ORANGE CHICKEN

Crispy coated chicken pieces served with a sweet, tangy orange sauce infused with aromatic sweet pickled ginger – this is the perfect dish when served on top of freshly steamed Thai fragrant rice.

3 MINUTES   **7 MINUTES**   **SERVES 2**

½ cup orange cordial
1 tsp custard powder
2 tbsp sugar
50g (½ cup) cornflour (cornstarch)
½ tsp salt
250g (9oz) diced chicken
(breast or thigh)
250ml (1 cup) vegetable oil
80g (3oz) pickled ginger
3–4 whole orange slices, to garnish

Combine the orange cordial, custard powder and sugar in a bowl, mix well and set to one side.

Mix the cornflour (cornstarch) and salt together in a bowl, then use to lightly coat the chicken pieces. Bang off the excess.

Heat the oil in a wok over a high heat and fry the chicken pieces for 4–5 minutes, stirring regularly to ensure even cooking and browning. Transfer the chicken to a wire rack or a plate lined with kitchen paper, then carefully tip the excess oil from the wok into a heatproof bowl to use in another recipe (once cool, strain to remove any cornflour residue).

Return the chicken to the wok, place back over a high heat and add the pickled ginger. Give the sauce mixture a stir to loosen it and pour into the wok. Bring the sauce to the boil, stirring continuously; once thickened, transfer to a serving plate. Garnish with the fresh orange slices and serve hot.

Kwoklyn's tip
Re-use the excess oil to make Chilli Chicken and Sesame Seeds (page 121), Garlic and Ginger Chicken (page 122), or Honey Chilli Chicken (page 130).

ROAST DUCK IN HOISIN SAUCE

Juicy slices of roast duck in a rich, dark hoisin sauce; all the flavour of a Chinese classic in a fraction of the time that it would take to roast a whole duck!

3 MINUTES   **7 MINUTES**   **SERVES 2**

1 tbsp vegetable oil
2 garlic cloves, grated
¼ whole deboned roasted Chinese duck, cut into slices (see Kwoklyn's tip)
75g (½ cup) sliced onion
1 bunch of spring onions (scallions), cut into 5cm (2in) slices
75g (½ cup) sliced bamboo shoots

For the sauce
60ml (¼ cup) chicken stock
3 tbsp hoisin sauce
1 tsp sugar
1 tsp dark soy sauce
½ tbsp Chinese rice wine (Shaoxing wine)
¼ tsp cornflour (cornstarch)

Combine the ingredients for the sauce in a bowl, mix well and set to one side.

Place a non-stick wok over a medium–high heat, add the oil and garlic and fry for a few seconds until fragrant. Next add the duck slices and fry for 1 minute, stirring throughout for even cooking. Add the sliced onion and continue to cook for a further 2 minutes.

Add the spring onions (scallions) and stir-fry for 30 seconds, then toss in the sliced bamboo shoots. Give the sauce mix a stir, add it to the wok and bring it all to the boil. Continue to cook for another minute or two to allow the sauce to thicken. Transfer to a serving plate and enjoy.

Kwoklyn's tip
Buy a whole deboned roasted Chinese duck from your local Asian supermarket and break it down into portions before storing in your freezer for use in other recipes.

HONEY CHILLI CHICKEN

Tender pieces of crispy coated chicken stir-fried with green spring onions in a sweet and spicy honey-chilli glaze.

2 MINUTES   **8 MINUTES**   **SERVES 2**

50g (½ cup) cornflour (cornstarch)
½ tsp salt
250g (9oz) diced chicken
   (breast or thigh)
250ml (1 cup) vegetable oil
150g (1 cup) diced onion
2 tsp ginger purée
5 spring onion (scallion) greens,
   roughly chopped on the diagonal
2 tbsp honey
1 tbsp fermented chilli bean paste
   (doubanjiang)
80ml (⅓ cup) lemon juice
½ tbsp light soy sauce

Mix the cornflour (cornstarch) and salt together in a large bowl, then lightly coat the chicken pieces with this seasoned flour and bang off the excess.

Heat the oil in a wok over a high heat and fry the coated chicken pieces for 4–5 minutes, stirring regularly to ensure even cooking and browning. Transfer the chicken to a wire rack or a plate lined with kitchen paper, then carefully tip the excess oil from the wok into a heatproof bowl to use in another recipe (once cool, strain to remove any cornflour residue).

Return the chicken to the wok, place back over a high heat, add the diced onion and ginger purée and cook for 1 minute, then add the spring onion (scallion) greens and cook for another 30 seconds. Add the remainder of the ingredients and continue to cook for a further 2 minutes. As soon as the sauce starts to bubble, give it a final stir and transfer to a serving plate.

Kwoklyn's tip
Re-use the excess oil to make Chilli Chicken and Sesame Seeds (page 121), Garlic and Ginger Chicken (page 122), or Ginger and Lemon Chicken (page 124).

ROAST DUCK WITH GREEN PEPPERS

This rich and uniquely savoury roast duck in black bean sauce is perfect heaped on a mound of freshly steamed jasmine rice.

4 MINUTES   **6 MINUTES**   **SERVES 2**

1 tbsp vegetable oil
2 tsp garlic purée
2 tsp ginger purée
¼ whole deboned roasted
   Chinese duck, cut into slices
   (see Kwoklyn's tip)
150g (1 cup) diced onion
1 tsp diced chilli
150g (1 cup) diced green
   (bell) pepper
80g (½ cup) sliced carrots
4 tbsp black bean sauce
   (you can also use black
   bean and garlic sauce)
pinch of white pepper
salt, to taste

Place a non-stick wok over a medium-high heat, add the oil and fry the garlic and ginger purées for a few seconds until fragrant. Add the duck slices and fry for 1 minute, stirring throughout for even cooking.

Add the onion and chilli and cook for a further 1 minute. Next add the green (bell) peppers and, after 30 seconds of stir-frying, add the sliced carrots and black bean sauce along with a pinch of white pepper and give everything a good stir. Taste for seasoning and add salt if required. Transfer to a serving plate.

Kwoklyn's tip
Buy a whole deboned roasted Chinese duck from your local Asian supermarket and break it down into portions before storing in your freezer for use in other recipes.

MONGOLIAN CHICKEN

Of Chinese-American origin, this dish is adapted from Mongolian Beef, a hugely popular dish in restaurants and takeaways, especially in the USA. Here, succulent pieces of chicken are cooked in a spicy sauce with beansprouts and tender spring onion greens. A perfect 10-minute treat for lunch, dinner or a late-night supper.

3 MINUTES   **7 MINUTES**   **SERVES 2**

2 tbsp vegetable oil
(or use sunflower)
150g (5oz) diced chicken
(breast or thigh)
150g (1 cup) diced onion
1 tsp chilli flakes
1½ tsp garlic purée
100g (2 cups) beansprouts
3–5 spring onions (scallions),
roughly chopped
1 tbsp Chinese rice wine
(Shaoxing wine)
1 tsp cornflour (cornstarch),
mixed with 2 tsp water
1 tsp sesame oil

For the sauce
2 tbsp hoisin sauce
1 tbsp dark soy sauce
2 tbsp oyster sauce
1 tsp sugar
½ tbsp rice vinegar

Combine the ingredients for the sauce in a bowl, mix well and set to one side.

Heat a non-stick wok over a high heat and add the vegetable oil. Once the wok begins to smoke, add the chicken and cook for 4–5 minutes until the chicken has browned on all sides and is cooked all the way through. Now add the diced onion, chilli flakes and garlic purée and cook for a further minute. Add the sauce mix to the wok and stir well to combine. Add the beansprouts, spring onions (scallions) and rice wine and give it all a good stir.

Give the cornflour (cornstarch) mixture a stir to loosen it and drizzle into the wok, making sure you keep the ingredients moving as you do this. Keep stirring until the sauce has thickened to the consistency of thick pouring cream (you may not need all of the mixture for this). Transfer to a serving dish and finish with a drizzle of sesame oil.

SMOKED CHILLI CHICKEN

Tender pieces of chicken are marinated in a crispy hoisin coating, tossed with sweet red peppers and fresh chillies and dressed in a smoky chilli bean sauce.

2 MINUTES   **8 MINUTES**   **SERVES 2**

2 tbsp hoisin sauce
250g (9oz) diced chicken
   (breast or thigh)
50g (½ cup) cornflour (cornstarch)
250ml (1 cup) vegetable oil
1 sweet red pointed pepper,
   chopped into 2cm (¾in)
   pieces on the diagonal
2–3 large red chillies, chopped into
   2cm (¾in) pieces on the diagonal
2 tsp garlic purée
1 tbsp sugar
1½ tbsp fermented chilli bean paste
   (doubanjiang)
½ tbsp rice vinegar
125ml (½ cup) water

In a large bowl, massage the hoisin sauce into the chicken pieces and then lightly coat them with the cornflour (cornstarch), banging off any excess.

Heat the oil in a wok over a high heat and fry the chicken pieces for 4–5 minutes, stirring regularly to ensure even cooking and browning. Transfer the chicken to a wire rack or a plate lined with kitchen paper, then carefully tip the excess oil from the wok into a heatproof bowl to use in another recipe (once cool, strain to remove any cornflour residue).

Return the chicken to the wok and place back over a high heat. Add the chopped sweet pepper and chillies and cook for 1 minute, then add the garlic purée. After 30 seconds add the remainder of the ingredients and cook for a further 1 minute. Once everything is well combined, transfer to a serving plate.

Kwoklyn's tip
Re-use the excess oil to make Chilli Chicken and Sesame Seeds (page 121), Garlic and Ginger Chicken (page 122), or Honey Chilli Chicken (page 130).

ROAST DUCK WITH MUSHROOMS

Here roast duck slices are served with your favourite mushrooms in a velvety smooth Chinese gravy.

3 MINUTES   **7 MINUTES**   **SERVES 2**

1 tbsp vegetable oil
2 garlic cloves, grated
¼ whole deboned roasted
   Chinese duck, cut into slices
   (see Kwoklyn's tip)
75g (½ cup) diced onion
75g (½ cup) sliced carrots
250g (4 cups) sliced mushrooms
1 tsp sesame oil

For the sauce
125ml (½ cup) chicken stock
2 tbsp oyster sauce
1 tsp sugar
1 tsp dark soy sauce
1 tbsp Chinese rice wine
   (Shaoxing wine)
½ tsp cornflour (cornstarch)

Combine the ingredients for the sauce in a bowl, mix well and set to one side.

Place a non-stick wok over a medium-high heat, add the vegetable oil and fry the garlic for a few seconds until fragrant, then add the duck slices and fry for 1 minute, stirring throughout for even cooking.

Add the onion and carrots and cook for a further 2 minutes. Now add the mushrooms and, after a further 1–2 minutes of cooking, give the sauce mix a stir, add to the wok and bring to the boil. Continue to cook for a further minute to allow the sauce to thicken, then remove from the heat. Transfer to a serving plate and drizzle with sesame oil.

Kwoklyn's tip
Buy a whole deboned roasted Chinese duck from your local Asian supermarket and break it down into portions before storing in your freezer for use in other recipes.

ZESTY LEMON CHICKEN

This dish of juicy chicken and mixed vegetables in a zingy lemon sauce cleanses your palate with every mouthful.

2 MINUTES   **8 MINUTES**   **SERVES 2**

1 tbsp vegetable oil
250–300g (9–10oz)
   chicken breast, sliced
1 tsp garlic purée
100g (⅔ cup) sliced carrots
200g (7oz) mangetout (snowpeas)
50g (2oz) pickled ginger
150g (2½ cups) sliced mushrooms
3 spring onions (scallions), sliced
   into 5cm (2in) slices

For the sauce
1 tsp grated lemon zest
3 tbsp lemon juice
250ml (1 cup) chicken stock
3 tbsp light soy sauce
2 tsp cornflour (cornstarch)

Combine the ingredients for the sauce in a bowl, mix well and set to one side.

Place a non-stick wok over a medium-high heat, add the oil and fry the sliced chicken for 2–3 minutes, stirring occasionally to ensure even browning. Next add the garlic purée and fry for a further 20 seconds before adding the carrots, mangetout (snowpeas), pickled ginger and mushrooms. Continue to stir-fry for a further 2 minutes.

Add the spring onions (scallions), then give the sauce mix a quick stir, add to the wok and bring to the boil, mixing the whole time. Continue to cook for a further 2 minutes to allow the sauce to thicken, then transfer to a serving plate.

NOODLES & RICE

BEEF NOODLES

Tender marinated strips of beef, vegetable slivers and crunchy beansprouts mingle together with springy egg noodles to deliver perfect mouthfuls.

5 MINUTES   **5 MINUTES**   **SERVES 2**

300g (10oz) beef fillet,
 cut into very thin slices
2 tbsp hoisin sauce
250ml (1 cup) vegetable oil
150g (1 cup) sliced onion
150g (1 cup) sliced carrots
pinch of salt
pinch of white pepper
pinch of sugar
300g (10oz) ready-to-wok egg
 noodles (2 nests)
200g (4 cups) beansprouts

For the sauce
2 tbsp oyster sauce
½ tbsp dark soy sauce
1 tbsp Chinese rice wine
 (Shaoxing wine)

Combine the ingredients for the sauce in a bowl, mix well and set to one side.

Place the beef into a bowl and massage with the hoisin sauce until well coated.

Heat the oil in a wok over a high heat and fry the beef pieces for 1 minute, stirring regularly to ensure even cooking and browning. Remove the beef with a slotted spoon and place on a wire rack or plate lined with kitchen paper to drain, then carefully tip the excess oil from the wok into a heatproof bowl to use in another recipe.

Place the wok back over a high heat, add the onion and carrots along with the salt, pepper and sugar and fry for 1 minute. Next add the ready-to-wok egg noodles and beansprouts and, after a further minute of cooking, add the beef.

Give the sauce mixture a quick stir and add to the noodles, continuing to stir-fry until all the ingredients are well combined and heated through. Transfer to a serving bowl and enjoy.

CRAB RICE

Delicate flakes of crab meat tossed through lightly seasoned fried rice.

4 MINUTES   **6 MINUTES**   **SERVES 2**

2 tbsp vegetable oil
150g (1 cup) diced onion
2 eggs, beaten
1 x 145g (5oz) can crab
   meat, drained
1 x 250g (9oz) packet
   cooked basmati rice
1 tbsp oyster sauce
pinch of salt
3 spring onions (scallions),
   finely chopped
drizzle of sesame oil

Place a non-stick wok over a medium-high heat, add the vegetable oil and fry the onion for 1–2 minutes, then add the beaten egg and stir gently, allowing the egg to set. As soon as the egg is cooked, add the crab meat and cook for a further 1 minute.

Add the rice and combine well, then add the oyster sauce, salt and half the spring onions (scallions). Once the rice is piping hot, transfer to a serving plate, drizzle with sesame oil and sprinkle with the remaining spring onions.

FRIED RICE NOODLES WITH VEGETABLES

Pile your bowl high with tangled rice noodles and shredded vegetables for a quick spicy snack.

4 MINUTES   **6 MINUTES**   **SERVES 2**

vegetarian

1½ tbsp vegetable oil
5 spring onions (scallions),
   cut into 5cm (2in) slices
2 tsp garlic purée
1 tsp ginger purée
1 tsp dried chilli flakes
150g (1 cup) sliced (bell) peppers
100g (⅔ cup) grated carrot
300g (10oz) ready-to-wok rice
   noodles
200g (4 cups) beansprouts
drizzle of sesame oil

For the sauce

1 tbsp oyster sauce or mushroom
   stir-fry sauce
½ tbsp light soy sauce
1 tbsp Chinese rice wine
   (Shaoxing wine)
1 tsp sugar

Combine the ingredients for the sauce in a bowl, mix well and set to one side.

Place a non-stick wok over a medium-high heat, add the vegetable oil and fry the spring onions (scallions) with the garlic and ginger purées and chilli flakes for 1 minute, stirring throughout for even cooking. Add the peppers and grated carrot and cook for 1 minute, then add the rice noodles and stir-fry for 2 minutes before adding the beansprouts; give everything a good mix.

Give the sauce mixture a stir and add to the wok, continuing to cook for a final minute to allow the sauce to coat all of the cooked ingredients. Remove from the heat, transfer to a serving plate and drizzle with sesame oil.

HOT BEAN NOODLES

Glass noodles, so named for their transparency when cooked, are perfect for a rich chilli bean dish, glistening in the bowl as they are adorned with the vibrant colour and flavours of the sauce.

4 MINUTES   **6 MINUTES**   **SERVES 2**

vegan

150g (5oz) dried mung bean
   (glass) noodles (about 3 nests)
1½ tbsp vegetable oil
5 spring onions (scallions),
   cut into 5cm (2in) slices
2 tsp garlic purée
1 tsp chilli flakes
200g (4 cups) beansprouts
drizzle of sesame oil

For the sauce

2 tbsp fermented chilli bean
   paste (doubanjiang)
2 tbsp water
1 tbsp Chinese rice wine
   (Shaoxing wine)
½ tbsp rice vinegar
1 tsp dark soy sauce
1 tsp sugar

Combine the ingredients for the sauce in a bowl, mix well and set to one side.

Cook the mung bean noodles in a saucepan of boiling water for 1–2 minutes until soft, then drain and set to one side.

While the noodles are boiling, place a non-stick wok over a medium-high heat, add the vegetable oil and fry the spring onions (scallions) with the garlic purée and chilli flakes for 1 minute, stirring throughout for even cooking. Add the beansprouts and cook for a further minute.

Give the sauce mix a stir and add to the wok along with the drained glass noodles. Continue to cook to allow the sauce to coat all of the ingredients. Remove from the heat, transfer to a serving plate and finally drizzle with sesame oil.

KING PRAWN UDON IN HOISIN SAUCE

Originating from China but now more recognized as a Japanese noodle, udon are a much thicker and often round form of noodle with a dense, chewy texture – perfect for stir-fry dishes and soups alike.

3 MINUTES   **7 MINUTES**   **SERVES 2–3**

300g (10oz) fresh udon noodles
   (about 2 nests)
2 tbsp vegetable oil
300g (10oz) raw king prawns (jumbo
   shrimp), peeled and deveined
150g (1 cup) diced onion
5 spring onions (scallions),
   cut into thin 5cm (2in) slices
80g (½ cup) sliced bamboo shoots
100g (1 cup) canned baby corn,
   quartered lengthways
½ tbsp sesame oil

For the sauce
1 tbsp Chinese rice wine
   (Shaoxing wine)
3 tbsp hoisin sauce
60ml (¼ cup) vegetable stock
2 tsp sugar

Combine the ingredients for the sauce in a bowl, mix well and set to one side.

Rinse the noodles under warm water to loosen them, then drain and set to one side.

Heat a non-stick wok over a medium-high heat, add the vegetable oil and fry the king prawns (jumbo shrimp) for 2 minutes, then add the onion, spring onions (scallions), bamboo shoots and baby corn, stir-frying for a further 3 minutes. Add the loosened udon noodles and continue to fry for another minute.

Give the sauce mix a quick stir, add to the wok and continue to fry until all of the ingredients are well combined and warmed through. Remove from the heat, stir in the sesame oil and transfer to warmed serving bowls.

MINCED PORK NOODLES

Sweet flecks of minced pork in a rich, spicy sauce, all wrapped around plump, chewy udon noodles.

4 MINUTES   **6 MINUTES**   **SERVES 2–3**

2 tbsp vegetable oil
200g (7oz) minced (ground) pork
5 spring onions (scallions),
    cut into thin 5cm (2in) slices
2 tsp garlic purée
200g (4 cups) beansprouts
300g (10oz) ready-to-wok
    udon noodles (about 2 nests)
drizzle of sesame oil

For the sauce
2 tbsp fermented chilli bean paste
    (doubanjiang)
2 tbsp yellow bean sauce
125ml (½ cup) chicken stock
1 tbsp Chinese rice wine
    (Shaoxing wine)
1 tsp dark soy sauce
1 tsp light soy sauce
2 tsp sugar

Combine the ingredients for the sauce in a bowl, mix well and set to one side.

Place a non-stick wok over a medium-high heat, add the vegetable oil and fry the pork for 2 minutes, mixing throughout to ensure even cooking. Add the spring onions (scallions) and the garlic purée and cook for a further 1 minute before adding the beansprouts.

Give the sauce mix a stir and add to the wok along with the udon noodles. Continue to cook, allowing the noodles to soften and the sauce to coat all of the ingredients. Remove from the heat, transfer to a serving plate and finish with a drizzle of sesame oil.

MUSHROOM NOODLES

In this recipe rich, earthy mushrooms, fresh peppery beansprouts and soft egg noodles are all smothered in a deep, dark umami-laden sauce.

4 MINUTES   **6 MINUTES**   **SERVES 2–3**

vegan

2 tbsp vegetable oil
150g (1 cup) sliced onion
2 tsp garlic purée
1 x 150g (5oz) can sliced
   mushrooms, drained
1 x 410g (14oz) can beansprouts,
   drained (or use 200g/4 cups
   fresh beansprouts)
300g (10oz) ready-to-wok
   egg noodles (about 2 nests)
drizzle of sesame oil

For the sauce
125ml (½ cup) vegetable stock
1 tbsp Chinese rice wine
   (Shaoxing wine)
1 tbsp mushroom stir-fry sauce
1 tsp sugar
1 tsp light soy sauce
1 tsp dark soy sauce
pinch of white pepper

Combine all the ingredients for the sauce in a bowl, mix well and set to one side.

Heat a non-stick wok over a medium-high heat, add the vegetable oil and fry the onion and garlic purée for 1 minute, then add the mushrooms and beansprouts and fry for another minute. Add the ready-to-wok noodles and cook for another minute, keeping everything moving in the wok.

Give the sauce mix a quick stir and add to the wok, continuing to stir-fry. Once the noodles have softened and are hot all the way through, transfer to a serving plate and drizzle with sesame oil.

SPAM® FRIED RICE

A popular breakfast dish in the street cafés of Hong Kong, this is fried rice with a twist. Since first hitting the shops in 1937 from its hometown of Austin, Minnesota, Spam® continues to grow in popularity, largely due to its long shelf life but also for its simply delicious flavour.

 4 MINUTES   **6 MINUTES**   **SERVES 2**

2 tbsp vegetable oil
½ x 170g (6oz) can Spam®,
   cut into bite-sized cubes
5 spring onions (scallions),
   thinly sliced
2 eggs, beaten
1 x 250g (9oz) packet
   cooked basmati rice
pinch of salt
drizzle of sesame oil

For the sauce
2 tbsp tomato ketchup
½ tbsp tomato purée (paste)
½ tbsp dark soy sauce
2 tbsp water

Combine the ingredients for the sauce in a small bowl, mix well and set to one side.

Place a non-stick wok over a medium-high heat, add the vegetable oil and fry the diced Spam® for 1 minute, then add half the spring onions (scallions) and fry for another minute.

Add the eggs and swirl the wok gently to allow the eggs to set, then add the rice along with a pinch of salt. Give it all a good mix and, once the rice has fried and is thoroughly heated, add the sauce mix and stir to combine with the rest of the ingredients. Transfer to a serving plate, drizzle with sesame oil and sprinkle over the remaining spring onions.

SWEET SOY BEEF NOODLES

Here thinly sliced beef fillet is gently poached in a sweet soy sauce with green spring onions.

4 MINUTES   **6 MINUTES**   **SERVES 2**

200g (7oz) dried flat rice noodles
125ml (½ cup) light soy sauce
60ml (¼ cup) mirin
1 tbsp sugar
3 spring onions (scallions), cut into
  2cm (¾in) slices on the diagonal
300g (10oz) beef fillet,
  cut into very thin slices
2 tsp ginger purée

Cook the flat noodles in a large saucepan of boiling water for 2 minutes until soft, then drain and set to one side.

Place a non-stick wok over a medium-high heat, add the soy sauce, mirin and sugar and bring to the boil. Add the spring onions (scallions) and cook for 1 minute, then add the thinly sliced beef and ginger purée. Stir for 20–30 seconds then add the drained noodles. Cook for 1 more minute, or until the noodles have warmed through, then transfer to a serving bowl.

Kwoklyn's tip
This dish is traditionally made using shirataki or mung bean (glass) noodles and is also known as 'waterfall noodles', as the thin and transparent shirataki noodles represent a cascading waterfall.

YELLOW BEAN FLAT RICE NOODLES WITH GREEN BEANS

Wide flat rice noodles (*ho fun*) and crisp green beans are lavishly adorned with an aromatic Chinese yellow bean sauce.

3 MINUTES   **7 MINUTES**   **SERVES 2**

vegan

200g (7oz) dried flat rice noodles
1½ tbsp vegetable oil
5 spring onions (scallions),
   cut into 5cm (2in) slices
1 tsp ginger purée
200g (7oz) green beans,
   cut into 2cm (¾in) lengths
200g (4 cups) beansprouts
drizzle of sesame oil

For the sauce
2 tbsp yellow bean sauce
2 tbsp water
1 tbsp Chinese rice wine
   (Shaoxing wine)
1 tsp dark soy sauce
1 tsp sugar

Combine the ingredients for the sauce in a bowl, mix well and set to one side.

Cook the flat noodles in a large saucepan of boiling water for 2 minutes until soft, then drain and set to one side.

While the flat rice noodles are boiling, place a non-stick wok over a medium-high heat, add the vegetable oil and fry the spring onions (scallions) with the ginger purée for 1 minute, stirring throughout for even cooking. Add the green beans and cook for 1 minute, then add the drained rice noodles and stir-fry for another minute. Finally add the beansprouts and mix everything together.

Give the sauce mixture a quick stir, add to the wok and continue to cook to allow the sauce to coat all of the other ingredients. Remove from the heat, transfer to a serving plate and finally drizzle with sesame oil.

INDEX

ACKNOWLEDGEMENTS

Wow, who would have thought I'd be writing my acknowledgement page for book number four! What a truly amazing journey that started long before I was even born.

My first thanks have to go to my grandad, who unfortunately I never got to meet, but from what I've been told, he was a wonderful man who favoured my dad, so I know he had to be the best. The courage it must have taken for my grandad to move his entire family to a country that he had never visited and then to start his own Chop Suey House is awe inspiring. I'd like to think his motto would have been 'If you can dream it, you can do it.' Thank you again, Grandad.

My wonderful mum and, of course, my amazing dad – what a team! To take on adversity as you did back in the late 60's and 70's is mind boggling (a story for another occasion). You are both truly amazing and I feel so lucky every single day to be your pain-in-the-backside son. I hope I've made you proud, as I feel so privileged to be able to share the skills that you taught me growing up in our little Chinese restaurant in Leicester.

Jo, if it wasn't for your proofreading, co-writing and general genius, I'd still be on book one now. You are truly awesome, and writing these books has been so much fun. Oh, and did I mention spelling mistakes? There'd be a lot, lot more spelling mistakes in the manuscript without you.

Clare Hulton (my agent), Sarah Lavelle (publisher) and the Quadrille team: it was you guys who gave me the chance to share my love of Chinese food through my books; you took a chance and I hope I've made you proud too. I could never thank you enough for the opportunity, but thank you anyway.

And last but by no means least, I cannot thank each and every one of you enough for following my journey and buying my books.